LORD, TEACH US TO PRAY

Living The Lord's Prayer

ROBERT GRIFFITH

GRACE AND TRUTH PUBLISHING
PO Box 338, Gunnedah NSW 2380 Australia
www.graceandtruthpublishing.com.au

ISBN 978-1-7635504-8-3

TABLE OF CONTENTS

The Lord's Prayer

Our Father in heaven,
hallowed be your name,
your kingdom come,
your will be done,
on earth as it is in heaven.
Give us today our daily bread.
and forgive us our sins,
as we forgive those who sin against us.
And lead us not into temptation,
but deliver us from the evil one.
For Yours is the kingdom,
the power and the glory,
for ever and ever, amen.

1. HOW NOT TO PRAY

Prayer is a universal expression of human longing. Across every religion and philosophy, people instinctively turn to something - or someone – that's beyond themselves in times of desperation, gratitude, or need. For the Christian, however, prayer is neither ritual nor routine - it is relationship. It is the living breath of our spiritual life.

Jesus' first disciples understood this well. They watched Jesus perform miracles, teach with divine authority, and confront the powers of darkness - and yet, of all the things they could have asked Him to teach them, they asked, *"Lord, teach us to pray."* (Luke 11:1). Why? Because they saw that Jesus' life was saturated with prayer. They saw Him retreat from crowds to be alone with the Father. They saw the deep connection between His prayers and His power. They longed to know the secret - and so do we.

However, before Jesus gave them the words of what we now call The Lord's Prayer, He gave them a lesson on how not to pray. That's where we must begin - because if our understanding of prayer is skewed, even our most sincere prayers can become ineffective or even harmful.

When you pray - not if you pray

Jesus begins His teaching in Matthew 6:5 with the words, *"And when you pray..."* Notice He didn't say, *"If you pray."* He said when you pray. Prayer is not optional for a disciple of Jesus; it is essential. Just as breathing is not an optional activity for our physical survival, so prayer is the spiritual oxygen of a believer's life. If we do not pray, we suffocate spiritually.

Therefore, Jesus assumes His followers will pray - it's part of the very fabric of discipleship. But He doesn't leave it there. He immediately calls out the common pitfalls: *"And when you pray, do not be like the hypocrites, for they love to pray standing in the synagogues and on the street corners to be seen by others. Truly I tell you, they have received their reward in full."* (Matthew 6:5)

Jesus exposes a dangerous tendency in religious people - using prayer as performance. The Pharisees of His day had turned prayer into a public spectacle, designed to impress others rather than commune with God. Their long, flowery prayers, loudly spoken in public places, may have sounded holy - but their audience was not God; it was the crowd. They weren't praying; they were performing.

Prayer is not a performance

There is a very fine line between public prayer and performative prayer. Jesus is not forbidding corporate prayer - after all, He prayed in public many times. What He condemns is the motive behind it. When our desire is to be seen rather than to seek, we have already missed the point. If people's applause is what we're after, Jesus says we'll get it - but that's all we will get.

This warning is deeply relevant for us today. Whether in church services, social media posts, or casual Christian conversation, it is possible to appear prayerful without being prayerful. Our culture, much like the ancient religious culture Jesus addressed, often confuses appearance with authenticity.

Jesus calls us back to reality: prayer is about intimacy with God, not impressing others. In contrast to the hypocrisy of public performance, Jesus offers a radical alternative: *"But when you pray, go into your room, close the door and pray to your Father, who is unseen. Then your Father, who sees what is done in secret, will reward you."* (Matthew 6:6)

Jesus is not simply giving architectural advice here. He's talking about posture - of the heart and of the body. He is calling us to private, sincere, focused communion with God. The *"room"* becomes a metaphor for withdrawing from distraction, from ego, from performance, and coming honestly before God.

The Father who *"is unseen"* meets us in the unseen places. And the reward is not money, success, or power. The reward is God Himself. It is relationship. It is the quiet, joyful assurance that God sees, hears, and loves us.

Instead of public approval, seek private communion. Instead of visible acts of piety, embrace unseen fellowship with God. In the original language, the word for *"room"* (*tameion*) refers to a small, inner chamber - a storage room or closet in a house, often without windows. It's the last place anyone would expect to have a spiritual encounter - and that's precisely the point.

God isn't found in the flashiness of external display. He is found in the hidden place. Secrecy in prayer protects sincerity. When no one is watching, you have no one to impress. You can drop the mask, the vocabulary, the script - and just be. There, in the hidden chamber, prayer becomes what it was always meant to be: a child talking to their Father.

Jesus says, *"Then your Father, who sees what is done in secret, will reward you."* (v. 6). What is that reward? It is not earthly applause. It is not public elevation. It is certainly not the fulfillment of every personal desire. The reward is Him. His presence. His peace. His nearness. There is something sacred about hidden obedience. When we pray and no one knows, when we intercede and no one hears, when we seek God with no thought of recognition - God sees - and He delights in that kind of faith.

It is worth asking ourselves: where is the secret place in our lives? Do we have a space - physical or spiritual - where we meet with God privately? If not, Jesus invites us to make that space. Not because prayer is location-dependent, but because our hearts need help entering stillness. In a world of endless noise and visibility, the quiet room becomes a sanctuary.

Prayer is not empty words

Jesus continues: *"And when you pray, do not keep on babbling like pagans, for they think they will be heard because of their many words."* (Matthew 6:7) This is the second danger in prayer: not just hypocrisy, but emptiness.

The word *"babbling"* in the Greek suggests mindless repetition or chatter. Jesus is critiquing the practice of piling up lots of phrases, mantras, or formulaic expressions in the vain hope of manipulating the God.

In ancient pagan religions, the more elaborate or repeated a prayer, the more likely the god would respond. But the God of Scripture is never manipulated by words. He is always moved by hearts.

The issue here is not repetition per se - after all, Jesus Himself repeated His prayers in Gethsemane (Matthew 26:44), and the Psalms are full of repeated refrains. The issue here is mindless repetition - empty words said out of superstition, ritual, or manipulation. In many pagan religions of the first century, prayer was a kind of verbal incantation. If you said the right words, the right number of times, in the right order, you could get the gods to act. Jesus says, *"That's not how our Father works."* The God of Israel - our Father - is not reluctant. He is not distant. He is not mechanical. He doesn't respond to formulas; He responds to faith.

This strikes at the heart of much modern prayer confusion. How often do we treat prayer like a transaction? If I say it just right, if I pray long enough, if I get enough people to join me, then surely God will listen. But Jesus tells us that our Father already knows. We don't need to persuade Him. We just need to trust Him.

In our context, this might mean reciting prayers by habit without thought or emotion, repeating Christian clichés, or using prayer as a means to control outcomes. The power of prayer is not in the quantity of words, but in the quality of trust. God is not a vending machine we manipulate - He is a Father we approach.

Your Father knows what you need

Jesus concludes this portion of teaching with a profound reminder: *"Do not be like them, for your Father knows what you need before you ask him."* (Matthew 6:8) What an astonishing truth! We do not inform God of anything when we pray. He is not waiting to be enlightened by our petitions. He already knows. He is not surprised by our fears, our needs, or our pain. He knows it all - and more than that, He cares. So why do we pray at all? Because prayer is not about conveying information. It's about cultivating relationship.

God knows what we need, but He still wants us to come to Him anyway - not because He's in any way uinformed, but because we are. Prayer aligns our hearts with His. It shapes us. It humbles us. It draws us into the flow of divine love and wisdom. Prayer is not for God's benefit - it's for ours. We are not updating Him on our circumstances. We are aligning our hearts with His will. We are expressing trust. We are opening the door for His grace to enter our situation.

Imagine a parent who knows what their child needs but still loves to hear them ask. Why? Because it shows connection. It fosters relationship. God always delights in our dependence, not because He needs it, but because it reflects reality: we need Him. Even in our most desperate prayers, when words fail and emotions overwhelm, God already knows. He is not waiting for eloquence. He is waiting for honesty. He is not impressed by our phrasing. He is moved by our faith.

There is tremendous freedom in this truth: *"your Father knows what you need before you ask."* You don't have to pretend, and you don't have to perform. You don't have to explain everything. You are known. Fully. And loved. This changes how we pray. We stop striving. We stop scripting. We come as children to a good Father. We bring our fears, our doubts, our needs, our praise - and we lay them before Him, trusting that He hears, understands, and will respond in perfect wisdom and love.

This also frees us from comparing our prayers to others. You don't need to sound like your pastor, your Bible study leader, or your favourite Christian author. God doesn't value style. He values sincerity. Your voice is enough. Your words are enough. You are enough - because He is your Father.

As we open this book on The Lord's Prayer, Jesus begins not with the words to say, but with the posture to hold. He strips away the illusions and calls us to sincerity, simplicity, and intimacy. Before we say, *"Our Father in heaven,"* we really need to understand Who we're speaking to - and why. Prayer is not about public displays or religious formulas.

It's about drawing near to the Father who already knows us, sees us, and longs to commune with us.

Relearning prayer in the way of Jesus

As we reflect on this Jesus' opening instruction about prayer, we really must ask ourselves: what kind of praying have we grown accustomed to? Have we unconsciously adopted the posture of performance, like the hypocrites? Have we slipped into the babbling repetition of the pagans, thinking that volume or frequency might twist God's arm? Before Jesus teaches what to pray, He confronts how and why we pray. And it's here that we find the greatest need for reformation - not in our methods, but in our hearts.

The disciples were not prayerless people. As Jewish men, they would have been raised on prayer. They would have recited the Shema (Deuteronomy 6:4) daily: *"Hear, O Israel: The Lord our God, the Lord is one."* They would have prayed many of the Psalms in the synagogue or in the temple courts. And yet, something about Jesus' prayer life stood out. He prayed differently – He prayed with authority, intimacy, and power. They saw in Him this deep communion with God that was dynamic. That's why they said, *"Lord, teach us to pray."*

Prayer is relational, not ritualistic

Prayer is not a religious hoop we jump through to gain spiritual credit. Nor is it a vending machine into which we insert the right spiritual coins. It is a relational conversation with the living God. At its core, prayer is not primarily about getting something from God, it's about connecting with God personally.

This is why Jesus consistently referred to God as Father. He was the first rabbi to do this with such intimacy. For the religious leaders of the time, God was holy and exalted - and indeed He is. But Jesus brought that majesty into relationship. *"Our Father in heaven"* bridges transcendence and intimacy. So, when you pray, remember you are not approaching a boss, a judge, or a bureaucrat. You are coming to your Father - the One Who made you, knows you, and loves you. That changes everything.

Before giving us a pattern to follow in prayer, Jesus gives us a heart posture we need to adopt. He strips away the falsehoods of performance and the futility of manipulation. He shows us that real prayer is always grounded in relationship - with a Father Who is unseen, but Who sees; Who is silent, but Who hears; Who is sovereign, but Who is near.

As we prepare to dive into The Lord's Prayer itself, we are reminded that prayer begins not with our words, but with His presence. Not with our wants, but with His will. It begins not with anxiety, but with assurance. Our Father already knows.

The contrast between religion and relationship

The way Jesus introduces The Lord's Prayer forces us to confront a critical truth: religious activity does not guarantee spiritual vitality. The Pharisees were masters of religious performance. They tithed, fasted, prayed, and followed the Law meticulously - and yet Jesus often rebuked them for their hypocrisy. Why? Because their hearts were far from God. *"These people honour me with their lips, but their hearts are far from me."* (Matthew 15:8)

That same danger exists today. We can go through the motions of Christian life - attend church activities, say prayers, even lead ministries - all while neglecting intimacy with God. Jesus begins His teaching on prayer by warning us that proximity to religious activity is never the same as relationship with the Father. Prayer is not ticking a box or earning favour. It is about communion - daily, honest, Spirit-led interaction with the living God. When we miss this, we reduce prayer to a ritual or a routine. But when we grasp it, prayer becomes the very heartbeat of our faith and our whole life!

Authentic prayer flows from a quiet confidence

The beauty of Jesus' teaching in Matthew 6:5-8 is its call to authenticity. True prayer doesn't need to be loud, lengthy, or impressive. It needs to be real. It needs to spring from a heart that knows who God is - a Father Who is near and loving - and who we are - children who are dependent and loved.

This leads to a kind of quiet confidence in prayer. You don't have to twist God's arm. You don't have to prove anything. You are already heard, already known, already loved. The Apostle Paul would later express this truth beautifully: *"In him and through faith in him we may approach God with freedom and confidence."* (Ephesians 3:12). Confidence in prayer doesn't come from eloquence or effort. It comes from knowing Jesus. He has torn the veil. He has opened the way. And through Him, we have access to the Father - not as beggars, but as sons and daughters.

Preparing the soil for the model prayer

All of this groundwork - Jesus' teaching about secrecy, sincerity, simplicity, and relationship, is not a detour, it's vital preparation. Jesus is tilling the soil of our hearts before planting the words of The Lord's Prayer. If our hearts are not right, the words will never take root. If our motives are off, even the most beautiful prayer becomes hollow.

Imagine trying to plant a seed in concrete. It won't grow. But when the soil is soft, rich, and ready, life can spring up. That's what Jesus is doing here. He is softening our hearts, correcting our posture, and preparing us to pray - not just with words, but with understanding. When Jesus finally says, *"This, then, is how you should pray..."* (Matthew 6:9), it is not a script to memorize - it's a way of life to embrace - a pattern built on the foundation He has just laid.

Prayer as formation, not just petition

There's one more truth we must grasp before we move into The Lord's Prayer itself: prayer is not just about making requests - it's about being formed. All too often, we treat prayer like some kind of divine wish list. *"God, please give me this... fix that... change them... open this door... close that one..."*

Of course, Scripture encourages us to bring our requests to God: *"Do not be anxious about anything, but in every situation, by prayer and petition, with thanksgiving, present your requests to God."* (Philippians 4:6). But that's not all prayer is. It is also the furnace in which our character is shaped.

In prayer, we are moulded into the likeness of Christ. In prayer, our will is aligned with God's will. In prayer, our desires are sifted, purified, and refined. When Jesus teaches us to pray, He is not only teaching us what to say - He is teaching us who to become.

The Father is always at the centre

Throughout this entire passage, Jesus repeatedly uses one key word to describe God: Father. This is the foundation upon which all else rests. Every instruction He gives - go into your room, don't babble, trust that you are being heard – all hinges on this relationship. And it's worth noting how revolutionary this was. In the Old Testament, God was very rarely addressed directly as Father. He was Creator, King, Lord of Hosts, the Holy One of Israel. Yet Jesus, the Son of God, invites us into His own intimacy with the Father. He doesn't just say, "*My Father.*"

He teaches us to say, "*Our Father.*" This is a staggering truth. The God Who made the whole universe invites us to call Him *Father*. Not in metaphor. Not in theory, but in reality.

Through Christ, we are adopted into His family: "*The Spirit you received brought about your adoption to sonship. And by him we cry, 'Abba, Father.'*" (Romans 8:15). This identity is foundational. If we don't understand that God is our Father, we will always pray from a place of fear, distance, or doubt. But when we truly grasp this truth, our prayers become confident, bold, and intimate. We pray not as outsiders, but as beloved children.

The beginning of a transformational journey

This chapter is the doorway into The Lord's Prayer - a gateway into not only a set of words, but a completely new understanding of what it means to live in constant communion with our Father in heaven. Jesus has taken care in Matthew 6:5–8 to recalibrate our assumptions. He shatters the performance-driven, works-based, superstitious models of prayer. In their place, He planted something beautiful: relational access to the Father, grounded in grace and fuelled by love. As we move forward into the prayer itself in the coming chapters, we must remember this foundation.

The prayer Jesus gives us is not magic. It is not mechanical. It is not a formula. It is an invitation - to know God, to be changed by Him, and to participate in His kingdom on earth.

Personal application: Where is your secret place?

So let us ask ourselves:

➤ Have I built a habit of private, intimate prayer with God?
➤ Have I allowed my prayer life to become performative, rather than personal?
➤ Am I striving to be heard, or am I resting in the truth that I am already known and loved?
➤ Do I see God primarily as my Father - or as someone I must impress?

The answers to these questions reveal much about the posture of our hearts. But the good news is this: no matter where we are today, Jesus is ready to teach us. Like the disciples, we can come to Him and say, *"Lord, teach us to pray."* And He will.

As we finish this first chapter in our journey through The Lord's Prayer, we are reminded that how we pray matters deeply to Jesus. Before He gave His disciples the words to say, He gave them - and us - the heart to carry them.

The Lord's Prayer is not just a model to recite. It is a doorway into the very heart of God. But to walk through it, we must leave behind the baggage of performance, manipulation, and self-reliance. We must enter the secret place. We must approach our heavenly Father with humility, confidence, and childlike trust. For this is the beginning of true prayer: not a duty, but a delight; not a formula, but a friendship; not a performance, but a posture of love.

2. 'OUR FATHER IN HEAVEN'

The first words that change everything

Jesus begins The Lord's Prayer with a profound phrase: *"Our Father in heaven..."* (Matthew 6:9a). At first glance, these words may seem ordinary. Many Christians have repeated them thousands of times in church services, at funerals, or in quiet devotion. But we must not mistake familiarity for simplicity. These four words contain a theological revolution. They invite us into a new way of relating to God - not as distant Deity, not as detached Judge, not as impersonal Force, but as our Father.

Before we ask for daily bread, forgiveness, or deliverance, Jesus anchors our entire prayer life in the truth of our relationship with God. Every petition that follows, flows from this opening address. If we fail to really understand this phrase, we will misunderstand everything that follows. Therefore, let us slow down, linger here, and explore what Jesus meant when He taught us to begin prayer with the words, *"Our Father in heaven."*

"Our" - The prayer of the community

Notice that the first word of The Lord's Prayer is not *"My,"* but *"Our."* That is very significant. Jesus, in teaching us how to pray, deliberately makes this a corporate prayer. He reminds us from the outset that we do not pray in isolation. Even when we pray privately, we do so as part of a community - the body of Christ, the family of God. Prayer is both personal and collective.

This word *"our"* reflects a deep spiritual truth: we are not alone. We belong to a larger story, a people redeemed by God and brought together as brothers and sisters in Christ. When we pray *"Our Father,"* we are joining with believers across the world and across time. We are uniting our voices with saints and martyrs, children and elders, churches and small groups - all addressing the same Father. This challenges the hyper-individualism of modern Western culture. Christianity is not a solo journey. Faith is lived out in community. Prayer, too, is an act of unity.

Even Jesus, when He taught this prayer, was including Himself in a fellowship with others. Though He was the unique Son of God, He spoke the language of solidarity: *Our* Father, and as Jesus, the man, identifies with us in prayer, how much more should we identify with one another?

"Father" - The heart of the relationship

The word *"Father"* is the most powerful and controversial word in this phrase. It was not common in Jewish prayers to address God so intimately. The Old Testament certainly acknowledges God as Father - but mainly as the Father of Israel as a nation (Isaiah 63:16). Rarely was God addressed as our personal Father in prayer. Jesus changes everything.

Throughout the Gospels, Jesus consistently refers to God as Father - and He invites His disciples to do the same. In fact, He chooses to us the Aramaic word *"Abba"* - an affectionate term akin to *"Dad"* or *"Papa."* It conveys the idea of closeness, trust, and love.

Paul later affirms this in Romans 8:15: *"The Spirit you received brought about your adoption to sonship. And by him we cry, 'Abba, Father.'"* This is the miracle of the gospel - that sinners, once alienated from God, can now call Him Abba. Through faith in Christ, we are adopted into the family of God. He is not just the Father - He is our Father.

But what kind of Father is He? He is not harsh or unpredictable. He is not emotionally distant or abusive. Sadly, many people struggle with the whole concept of God as Father because of painful earthly experiences. Jesus wants to redeem that picture. He reveals a Father who is kind, trustworthy, generous, holy, and always near.

In the parable of the prodigal son (Luke 15), Jesus gives us a picture of the Father who runs to welcome His child home. This is the heart of God. He is not reluctant to receive us. He is eager. The moment we turn to Him in prayer, He meets us with compassion.

Fatherhood – The children of God

To call God Father implies something about us too: we are *His children*. This is not a universal status. While God is Creator of all, He is only Father to those who come to Him through Christ. John makes this clear: *"Yet to all who did receive him, to those who believed in his name, he gave the right to become children of God."* (John 1:12)

Prayer, then, is a family conversation. It's not a stranger trying to gain an audience with a monarch. It's a son or daughter walking into their Father's room - without fear, without hesitation, with love. And this identity as children of God changes everything. It means we pray not to earn acceptance, but from a place of acceptance. We don't grovel before a tyrant - we run to a Father who has already made space for us at His table.

This is why Jesus warns in Matthew 6:7 that prayer is not about heaping up words to be heard. Pagan gods always needed to be persuaded. Our Father does not. He already knows what we need before we ask. And He already loves us beyond measure.

Our assurance as children of God

Paul writes in Romans 8:16: *"The Spirit himself testifies with our spirit that we are God's children."* That inner witness is what makes prayer truly come alive. It's not a performance; it's a relationship. And the Holy Spirit reassures us that we belong to God - even when we feel distant, dry, or doubting. It's important to stress this because there are many believers who struggle with feelings of unworthiness. We think, *"God doesn't want to hear from me. I haven't been faithful. I've failed."* But this is where the doctrine of adoption is so powerful. You are not a child of God because of your performance. You are a child of God because of Christ's performance. And in Him, you are welcomed, loved, and heard. So, when Jesus teaches us to say, *"Our Father,"* He is not giving us a title - He is inviting us into a whole new identity.

With just two words - *"Our Father"* - Jesus now opens a door into a whole new world. A world of community, family, relationship, and identity.

It's a world where God is not distant but near, not angry but loving, not indifferent but involved. These words are more than an introduction to a prayer. They are a declaration of who we are and who God is. He is our Father - and we are His children.

"In Heaven" - The majesty of our Father

So far, we have explored the relational closeness of God as our Father. But Jesus immediately follows this intimate title with a crucial qualifier: *"in heaven."* These two words preserve the tension of the Christian life - intimacy and reverence, closeness and awe. To call God *"our Father in heaven"* is to anchor our prayer in both love and holiness. He is not just a father like any other. He is not bound by earthly limitations or human flaws. He is transcendent. He is above. He is sovereign. This phrase *"in heaven"* reminds us of His exalted position. He is enthroned above creation, ruling in perfect wisdom and power.

The psalmist declared: *"The Lord has established his throne in heaven, and his kingdom rules over all."* (Psalm 103:19). This is the God to Whom we pray - not merely a benevolent parent, but the King of the universe. And yet, He invites us to call Him Father.

Balancing nearness and transcendence

The great danger in our spiritual lives is veering too far in either direction - becoming too casual with God or too distant from Him. On the one hand, if we only emphasize God as our Father, we risk sentimentalism. God becomes like a friendly grandfather in the sky - warm and loving but lacking authority. Our prayers become shallow, self-centred, and even flippant. On the other hand, if we focus only on God as the transcendent Being *"in heaven,"* we risk fear and detachment. We may feel too small, too sinful, or too unworthy to pray at all. We can treat prayer like approaching a royal court, fearful of missteps.

Jesus holds both truths together: He is our Father - approachable, loving, compassionate. He is in heaven – all powerful, majestic, and holy. The tension is not a contradiction; it is a holy balance.

It keeps our prayers tender but reverent, intimate but respectful. This dual reality is beautifully captured in Ecclesiastes 5:2: *"God is in heaven and you are on earth, so let your words be few."* In other words, pray with love - and with awe.

Heaven as the place of power and perspective

To say that God is *"in heaven"* is not just to name His location - it's to affirm His authority. In biblical language, heaven is the seat of divine rule. It is the place from which God sees all, knows all, and governs all. When we pray to *"our Father in heaven,"* we are praying to the One Who sees the end from the beginning. The One Who is not caught off guard by global crises or personal tragedies. The One Who is never overwhelmed, never under-resourced and never confused. This brings profound comfort. When life on earth feels chaotic, we remember that our Father reigns from heaven. When our prayers seem weak, we remember they rise to a sovereign throne.

Isaiah 66:1 puts it plainly: *"This is what the Lord says: 'Heaven is my throne, and the earth is my footstool.'"* That is the God Who hears you when you pray. And that perspective changes the way we pray. We are not tossing words into the void. We are speaking to the God Who reigns over galaxies and nations yet bends to listen when His children whisper His name.

Reverence in the age of casual faith

In today's world, the concept of reverence is fading. We live in an age of informality. People wear pyjamas to the supermarket. We address CEOs by their first names. Social media platforms allow us to publicly criticize anyone, from politicians to popes. While informality can be good at times - breaking down barriers and encouraging honesty - it becomes dangerous when we bring it into our relationship with God in the wrong way. Reverence is not rigidity, but recognition. It is the humble acknowledgment that God is not like us. He is high and lifted up.

When we say, *"in heaven,"* we are reminded that He is holy. His ways are always higher than our ways. His thoughts are not our thoughts. He is not our equal. He is not obligated to us.

And yet, in His mercy, He loves us. Reverence is not fear that drives us away. It is awe that draws us near with the correct posture. Hebrews 12:28-29 says: *"Let us be thankful, and so worship God acceptably with reverence and awe, for our 'God is a consuming fire.'"* To call God *"our Father in heaven"* is to bow our hearts even as we lift our eyes.

Heaven as our hope and destination

There's another reason *"in heaven"* matters. It points us forward. Heaven is not just where God reigns - it is where His will is fully done. It is the realm of perfection, peace, righteousness, and joy. And for every believer, it is home. When we say, *"Our Father in heaven,"* we are not only recognizing where He is - we are also affirming where we belong. Philippians 3:20 reminds us: *"But our citizenship is in heaven. And we eagerly await a Saviour from there, the Lord Jesus Christ."*

This heavenly orientation shifts our desires and priorities. Earth is not our final destination. Our prayers are shaped by eternity. We pray not just for comfort now, but for the coming of God's kingdom. We pray with the long view in mind. When you feel weary, frustrated, or just overwhelmed by the brokenness of this world, remember this: your Father is in heaven - and He is preparing a place for you. Jesus said in John 14:2-3: *"My Father's house has many rooms... I am going there to prepare a place for you."*

Bringing Heaven to earth

One of the greatest tensions in the Christian life is this: we live on earth, but our Father is in heaven. We live in the broken *"now,"* but we long for the perfect *"not yet."* And yet Jesus teaches us to live - and pray - in light of heaven. The next line of The Lord's Prayer is: *"Your kingdom come, your will be done, on earth as it is in heaven."* (Matthew 6:10).

In other words, don't just gaze at heaven - pray it into reality here and now. Bring the values of heaven into your work, your home, your church, your neighbourhood. Pray and live in such a way that the glory of your Father in heaven becomes visible on earth.

When we start with *"Our Father in heaven,"* we are reminded that prayer is not just an escape - it is engagement. We are not praying to leave earth, but to see heaven's beauty reflected here.

The phrase *"Our Father in heaven"* is a masterpiece of theological balance. It joins intimacy with authority, love with majesty, nearness with transcendence. We approach God as children - but we do not forget that our Father is also on the throne. He is not small. He is not weak. He is not unaware. He is in heaven - and from that place of sovereign power, He hears all our cries. As we continue in this prayer, we do so with confidence and reverence, because our Father, Who reigns in heaven, has invited us to speak.

Living in the light of the Father's nature

Understanding that God is our Father in heaven is not just about how we pray - it's about how we live. If we truly believe that we are children of a heavenly Father, it changes our identity, our security, our obedience, and even our relationships with other people. The Lord's Prayer does not merely shape our petitions; it redefines our posture in the world.

The Apostle John reflects on this wonder in his first letter: *"See what great love the Father has lavished on us, that we should be called children of God! And that is what we are!"* (1 John 3:1). This truth should really astonish us. It should ignite joy, confidence, and humility. God has not simply allowed us to speak to Him - He has made us part of His family. He has not simply tolerated our presence - He delights in it.

But with this relationship comes responsibility. Children of the Father must reflect the Father. We are called to display His character in all things - His holiness, His compassion, His justice, His mercy. Jesus says in the Chapter on the Mount: *"Be perfect, therefore, as your heavenly Father is perfect."* (Matthew 5:48). This doesn't mean moral flawlessness. It means maturity, wholeness, and consistency in character. Just as our Father is gracious and faithful, we are to be gracious and faithful. Just as He is merciful, we are to show mercy.

Trusting the Father in times of uncertainty

If God is our Father in heaven, then we can trust Him - even when life feels chaotic. There will be seasons when His plans are unclear, His timing might seem delayed to us, and His ways feel mysterious. But knowing Who He is - and where He is - gives us strength. Jesus modelled this kind of trust. That night in the Garden of Gethsemane, He prayed: *"My Father, if it is possible, may this cup be taken from me. Yet not as I will, but as you will."* (Matthew 26:39). Here is the Son entrusting Himself fully to the Father – in spite of His agony. He does not approach God with detachment, but with intimacy and surrender. He says *"Father,"* even while trembling. In our pain, we can do the same.

We may not understand God's plan, but we know His heart. He is our Father and He is in heaven - which means He sees more than we can, knows more than we do, and rules with love that is perfect and pure. This kind of trust anchors us through suffering, doubt, and delay. It turns our prayers from panic to peace.

Unity under one Father

The first word of The Lord's Prayer is *"Our"* - and it is worth returning to it now as we consider its implications for the church. When we say, *"Our Father,"* we are really acknowledging that every Christian, regardless of race, background, denomination, or personality - shares the same spiritual Father. We are not just God's children individually; we are His family corporately. This means The Lord's Prayer is a call to unity.

In a world fractured by division, tribalism and suspicion, the Church should be a countercultural community of grace. When we gather to pray, whether in a cathedral or a living room, we are brothers and sisters. We are bound together, not by preferences or politics, but by blood - the blood of Jesus - and by the Spirit of adoption. Paul affirms this in Ephesians 4:4-6: *"There is one body and one Spirit... one Lord, one faith, one baptism; one God and Father of all, who is over all and through all and in all."* If God is our Father, we must learn to treat His other children with love, honour, and patience. We don't get to choose our siblings - but we are commanded to love them.

The privilege and responsibility of addressing God

One of the greatest privileges in life is being able to say, *"Our Father in heaven."* It is a phrase that angels dare not use. It is a title reserved for the redeemed. And yet, how casually we sometimes treat it. How easily we rush through the words without awe. But if we truly understood the access we've been given, our hearts would overflow with gratitude.

Hebrews 4:16 exhorts us: *"Let us then approach God's throne of grace with confidence, so that we may receive mercy and find grace to help us in our time of need."* This is the invitation of the gospel: to draw near to the throne - not as beggars or strangers, but as children. And not timidly, but boldly. Because our Father is both gracious and glorious.

But this privilege also comes with responsibility. To say *"Our Father in heaven"* is to align ourselves with His purposes. It's not a sentimental phrase – it is actually a powerful declaration of allegiance. We are not just asking for His help; we are purposely committing to His will.

Preparing to pray the rest of the prayer

This opening phrase is the foundation for everything that follows in The Lord's Prayer. Each petition - *"hallowed be your name," "your kingdom come," "give us today our daily bread,"* and so on - only makes sense in light of Who we are praying to. If God were not our Father, we would fear to ask for daily bread. If He were not in heaven, we would doubt His ability to deliver us. But because He is both, we pray with reverent confidence.

In many ways, the rest of The Lord's Prayer is a response to this opening line. We pray, *"hallowed be your name,"* because He is our holy Father. We pray, *"your will be done,"* because His will is perfect. We pray, *"deliver us from evil,"* because our Father in heaven is our defender.

So before we move on in this study to the next phrase of the prayer, we must let this one settle deeply into our hearts: He is our Father - and He is in heaven.

When Jesus taught His disciples to pray, He began with these words: *"Our Father in heaven..."* (Matthew 6:9a). He could have said *"Almighty Creator," "Sovereign Lord,"* or *"Righteous Judge."* All of those would have been true. But He chose *"Our Father."* And He invited us to say it too.

This phrase is not a formality. It is a theological declaration. It is the heartbeat of Christian prayer. It reminds us of Who God is - our loving, sovereign, holy Father. It reminds us of who we are - His beloved children. And it reminds us that we are part of a vast family, gathered from every tribe and tongue, all crying out to the same God.

As we continue through this prayer in the coming chapters, let us never lose sight of this foundation. Every request we bring - for His kingdom, for daily bread, for forgiveness, for deliverance - begins with this bold, beautiful truth:

He is our Father in heaven.

3. 'HALLOWED BE YOUR NAME'

The first request in The Lord's Prayer

After addressing God as *"Our Father in heaven,"* Jesus now leads us into the first petition of The Lord's Prayer: *"Hallowed be your name."* (Matthew 6:9b). This is not a phrase we use very often in everyday conversation. The word *"hallowed"* has an ancient, and almost mysterious ring to it. It feels formal, even distant. Yet Jesus places this as the very first request - before daily bread, before forgiveness, before guidance and protection. This is no accident. It reveals something deeply important about how we ought to pray, and more importantly, how we ought to live.

Jesus is teaching us that before we ask God for anything, we must first exalt Him for Who He is. Prayer should not begin with our needs; it should begin with God's glory - and that glory is most clearly seen in His name - His revealed identity, His character, His fame, and His reputation. To pray *"Hallowed be your name"* is to cry out from the heart, *"May Your name be honoured, revered, glorified, and set apart - not just in the world, but in my life."* This is worship before petition. Reverence before request. Adoration before asking. It then sets the tone for everything else.

What does "hallowed" mean?

The word *"hallowed"* is the Greek verb *hagiazō*, which means *"to make holy,"* *"to set apart,"* or *"to revere as sacred."* It's exactly the same root word used throughout the whole New Testament for *"sanctify"* or *"consecrate."* But in this case, it doesn't imply making God's name holy - as if it weren't already - rather, it is a request that His name be treated as holy. We are not changing God's character with our prayers. We are praying that the world - and our own hearts - would recognize and honour the holiness that is already His.

This is an important appeal that God's name would be glorified, exalted, and held in highest esteem - that it would not be used casually, misrepresented, or ignored, but revered with awe and wonder.

The Name of God: More than a label

In Scripture, a person's name is more than just an identifier. It reveals something about their nature, their essence. This is especially true of God. When Jesus says, *"Hallowed be your name,"* He's referring not just to the word *"God,"* but to everything God has revealed about Himself. God's name stands for His character, His reputation, His actions, and His presence. Throughout the Scriptures, God reveals His name to draw people into a deeper relationship. Each name is a window into God's character. And Jesus teaches us to pray that these names - and all they represent - would be honoured. Consider just a few examples:

➤ **Yahweh** - *"I AM WHO I AM"* (Exodus 3:14)
  The self-existent, eternal God.

➤ **El Shaddai** - *"God Almighty"* (Genesis 17:1)
  The all-powerful sustainer.

➤ **Jehovah-Jireh** - *"The Lord Will Provide"* (Genesis 22:14)
  The God Who meets our needs.

➤ **Jehovah-Rapha** - *"The Lord Who Heals"* (Exodus 15:26)
  The restorer of brokenness.

➤ **Jehovah-Shalom** - *"The Lord is Peace"* (Judges 6:24)
  The One Who brings wholeness.

Revering God's name in a culture of profanity

We live in a world where reverence is rare and God's name is often misused. It is invoked carelessly in conversation. It is shouted in anger or used as an exclamation. It is mocked in movies and memes. Even among believers, God's name can be handled flippantly - reduced to a cliché, a slogan, or a fallback in crisis. This is not a small matter.

The third commandment says: *"You shall not misuse the name of the Lord your God, for the Lord will not hold anyone guiltless who misuses his name."* (Exodus 20:7). This command isn't just about profanity. It's about treating God lightly - reducing His holy name to something common or trivial.

To *"hallow"* His name is to push against this cultural current and say: God is not ordinary. He is holy. His name is sacred. When we pray *"Hallowed be your name,"* we are committing ourselves to a life of honour - a life in which God's name is lifted up in our speech, our actions, our worship, and our decisions.

The name and the mission

Jesus connects God's name to His mission. In John 17, as He prays before going to the cross, He says: *"I have revealed you to those whom you gave me out of the world."* (v.6). *"I have made You known to them, and will continue to make You known..."* (v.26). In the original Greek, this is literally: *"I have revealed your name."* Jesus' life and ministry were all about making the Father known, displaying His character, revealing His heart, and glorifying His name.

This is the heartbeat of all Christian mission. We do not simply go into the world to relieve suffering, defend truth, or teach morality - we go to hallow the name of God. We exist to display His holiness, reflect His character, and spread the recognition of His name. That's why Jesus placed this request first in The Lord's Prayer. It's the foundation. Before we seek our needs to be met, we seek His name to be lifted high. Before we ask God to fix the world, we ask that His name be rightly known in the world.

Praying for the glory of God

"Hallowed be your name" is a prayer of worship - and it is also a prayer of alignment. We are asking God to do something in us, not just around us. We are saying, *"Let your name be honoured - beginning with me. Let it be hallowed in my words, my choices, my relationships, my work, my prayers."* In this light, the first petition becomes a prayer of surrender. We are saying, *"God, may my life be a platform for your glory. May your name be magnified in the way I forgive, the way I spend money, the way I raise children, the way I love my enemies, the way I suffer, the way I rejoice."* This is not a small prayer. It is the most expansive and radical prayer we could ever pray. It is asking God to reorient our desires, reshape our values, and reorder our priorities around His glory - not our own.

When Jesus teaches us to pray, *"Hallowed be your name,"* He is calling us to lift our eyes from our needs to God's glory. He is inviting us to begin prayer not with a shopping list, but with a song of praise. He is teaching us that the ultimate purpose of life - and of prayer - is to honour God. This simple phrase, though often overlooked, is a powerful daily reminder: God is holy. His name is sacred - and my highest calling is to revere Him with all that I am.

When God's Name is not hallowed

To truly grasp the weight of this prayer, we must consider the opposite. What does it look like when God's name is not hallowed? Scripture gives us many examples of times when people treated God's name as common or profane. One of the most sobering stories is in Leviticus 10, when Aaron's sons, Nadab and Abihu, offered *"unauthorized fire"* before the Lord - something He had not commanded. As priests, they had a responsibility to represent God's holiness, but they acted presumptuously.

The result was swift judgment: *"So fire came out from the presence of the Lord and consumed them, and they died before the Lord."* (Leviticus 10:2). God then says: *"Among those who approach me I will be proved holy; in the sight of all the people I will be honoured."* (Leviticus 10:3). The holiness of God is not just theoretical. It has real consequences. When His name is treated casually, or worse - misused, twisted, or commercialised - it dishonours His glory and misleads people.

In Ezekiel 36, God rebukes Israel for profaning His name among the nations. Their disobedience and idolatry caused the surrounding peoples to mock the God of Israel. God promises to act - not because His people deserved it, but to vindicate His name: *"I had concern for my holy name, which the people of Israel profaned among the nations where they had gone... I will show the holiness of my great name, which has been profaned among the nations, the name you have profaned among them."* (Ezekiel 36:21,23). This is crucial: God is passionate about the honour of His name.

He will act to uphold His glory - not because He is insecure, but because His name represents truth, righteousness, and life. To misrepresent Him is to distort the very foundation of reality.

Hallowing His name in our worship

One of the most immediate ways we can hallow God's name is through our worship. When we gather as the church - in homes, chapels, auditoriums, or cathedrals - we are coming not to be entertained, but to honour God. Worship is not a warm-up to the chapter. It is not an emotional experience for our benefit. It is a holy act of reverence. It is hallowing the name of our Father.

The Psalms are filled with calls to honour the name of the Lord: *"Ascribe to the Lord the glory due his name; worship the Lord in the splendour of his holiness."* (Psalm 29:2) *"Glorify the Lord with me; let us exalt his name together."* (Psalm 34:3). These verses show us that worship is not about preference - it is about posture. Whether we sing old hymns or modern songs, the goal is the same: to lift high the name of God.

But this is not limited to singing. Our entire gathering - from the prayers to the preaching to the way we interact with one another - should reflect reverence for God's name. When worship revolves around performance, popularity, or production value alone, we risk treating what is holy as common. To hallow God's name means we centre our gatherings around His glory - not our comfort or personal preference.

Hallowing His name in our words

Beyond worship services, we also hallow or profane God's name with our everyday speech. James addresses the inconsistency of blessing God with our mouths while cursing others: *"With the tongue we praise our Lord and Father, and with it we curse human beings... Out of the same mouth come praise and cursing. My brothers and sisters, this should not be."* (James 3:9–10). When we speak, we reveal what we believe about God. If we honour His name on Sunday but gossip, slander, and lie on Monday, then we are not hallowing His name - we are misrepresenting it.

Jesus warned that we will give account for every careless word (Matthew 12:36). That includes how we speak about God, how we use His name, and how we reflect His character in our language. This applies to how we talk to others and also how we talk about God - both in reverence and in truth.

Every preacher, teacher, and church leader, bears an even greater responsibility. We must speak of God with accuracy, humility, and honour, making sure we never use His name for personal gain or manipulation.

Hallowing His name in our conduct

Ultimately, our lives are the loudest proclamation of whether or not we hallow God's name. When we claim the name Christian, we are carrying the name of Christ. What we do, how we treat people, how we respond to trials - all of it either honours or dishonours God's name. Jesus said: *"Let your light shine before others, that they may see your good deeds and glorify your Father in heaven."* (Matthew 5:16).

This is a beautiful image of what it means to hallow God's name: to live in such a way that people are drawn to the God we serve. When we forgive generously, love sacrificially, serve humbly, and walk in integrity, we are reflecting our holy Father.

The opposite is also true. When Christians act with hypocrisy, greed, or cruelty, it damages the reputation of God. Gandhi famously said, *"I like your Christ. I do not like your Christians. Your Christians are so unlike your Christ."*

We cannot separate the holiness of God's name from the holiness of our lives. As His children, we are called to be living billboards for His glory.

A Prayer to live by His name

To pray *"Hallowed be your name"* is not just a request - it is a bold commitment. It is a strong declaration that we want our lives to be vessels of honour.

It is a prayer that says:

➢ May Your name be honoured in my home.
➢ May Your name be honoured in my parenting.
➢ May Your name be honoured in my workplace.
➢ May Your name be honoured in my choices, my conversations, and even my internet browsing.

So this prayer moves us from the theoretical to the practical. It shapes how we speak, how we spend, how we vote, how we work, how we treat others, and how we pursue holiness. It is a dangerous prayer - because it invites God to purify us. But it is also a beautiful prayer - because it leads us into the life we were created for: a life of honouring our Father in heaven.

"Hallowed be your name" is not just a line in a prayer - this is a lifelong pursuit. It is the lens through which we view worship, speech, conduct, and mission. It is a reminder that God's glory is the goal of our lives, and His name is the banner over all we do. As we allow these words to shape us, we begin to live differently. We become people who do not use God for our ends, but who exist for His glory. We become reflections of His holiness in a world that desperately needs to see what it means to live in awe of the living God.

When we don't feel like hallowing His name

Let's be totally honest here - there are times in life when it feels really difficult to hallow God's name. We can be overwhelmed, discouraged, angry, or just numb. Sometimes we are walking through personal pain. Other times, we are watching injustice in the world and wondering where God is. In those moments, we may not feel like lifting His name in praise. We may even feel distant from Him. But this is where The Lord's Prayer offers us a gift - it teaches us to pray not from our feelings, but from our faith. When we say, *"Hallowed be your name,"* we are not always declaring how we feel - we are declaring what we believe. We are anchoring ourselves in the truth of God's character, even when our emotions are stormy.

We are choosing to exalt His name above our circumstances. The Psalms give us a powerful model of this: *"Why, my soul, are you downcast? Why so disturbed within me? Put your hope in God, for I will yet praise Him, my Saviour and my God."* (Psalm 42:5). There's the key: *"I will yet praise Him."* That's what it means to hallow God's name in the dark - to say, *"Even now, even here, You are holy, and I will honour you."*

Hallowing God's name in a hostile world

We live in a cultural moment that is increasingly hostile or indifferent to the things of God. His name is often mocked, dismissed, or distorted. Biblical truth is seen as offensive. The church is scrutinized - sometimes fairly, often unfairly.

In such a climate, how do we hallow God's name? First, we do not retreat in fear or shrink back in shame. We stand firm in truth, but we do so with gentleness and humility.

Peter urges us: *"But in your hearts revere Christ as Lord. Always be prepared to give an answer... But do this with gentleness and respect."* (1 Peter 3:15). To hallow God's name in a hostile world is to live in such a way that our lives speak louder than our words. It is to hold fast to our convictions without becoming combative.

It is to love boldly and serve generously, so that even those who oppose us might take notice. Paul writes to the Philippians: *"Then you will shine among them like stars in the sky as you hold firmly to the word of life."* (Philippians 2:15-16). Hallowing God's name means reflecting His light into the darkness - not by yelling at the darkness, but by simply shining.

Hallowing God's name in prayer and practice

So how do we actually hallow God's name in daily life? Here are four simple but powerful ways:

1. *By Honouring His Word:* When we cherish, study, and obey Scripture, we are declaring that God's truth matters more than human opinion. We are hallowing His revealed will.

2. *By Trusting His Promises:* When we choose faith over fear, hope over despair, and obedience over convenience, we are saying, *"God, your name is trustworthy."* That honours Him.

3. *By Confessing Our Sin:* When we admit our failures and run to His mercy, we demonstrate that His holiness is real - and that His grace is sufficient. Honest confession hallows His name more than shallow perfection ever could.

4. *By Pointing Others to Him:* Every time we share the gospel, encourage a fellow believer, or explain why we live differently, we are lifting up His name before others.

Remember Jesus' words in John 12:32: *"And I, when I am lifted up from the earth, will draw all people to myself."* While that referred primarily to the cross, it reflects a spiritual principle: When we exalt Christ, people are drawn to Him.

The glory of God in all things

To pray *"Hallowed be your name"* is to embrace the central purpose of all creation - to glorify God. The prophet Habakkuk gives us this vision: *"For the earth will be filled with the knowledge of the glory of the Lord as the waters cover the sea."* (Habakkuk 2:14). This is where history is headed. As Paul said in Philippians 2, one day, every knee is going to bow and every tongue confess that Jesus Christ is Lord. On that day, God's name will be fully hallowed across heaven and earth. But we don't just wait for that day to begin. We start right now. We hallow God's name not just on Sundays, but in school drop-offs, staff meetings, quiet evenings at home, and conversations with neighbours.

Every moment is an opportunity to live for His glory. Paul put it this way: *"So whether you eat or drink or whatever you do, do it all for the glory of God."* (1 Corinthians 10:31)

A life that hallows God's name

As we conclude this chapter, the question now becomes deeply personal: Am I living in a way that hallows God's name? Let me make that more specific as we ask ourselves:

- ➢ Is His name honoured in my thoughts, speech, and habits?
- ➢ Do my relationships reflect His grace and truth?
- ➢ Does my use of time, money, and energy to glorify Him?
- ➢ Do I approach worship with reverence and awe?
- ➢ Do I confess sin quickly and rely on His mercy daily?

None of us does this perfectly. But the good news is that Jesus already has. He lived a life that perfectly hallowed the Father's name - and then He gave that life for us, so that we could be forgiven, adopted, and empowered to do the same. Because of Christ, we can now pray this prayer not as beggars, but as beloved children - children who long to see their Father's name lifted high in every corner of their lives and in every corner of the world.

Conclusion

"Hallowed be your name." This is not a passive hope. It is an active pursuit. It is the heartbeat of worship, the fuel of mission, and the mark of true discipleship. It is the cry of the redeemed who have seen the holiness of God and want His name to be known, loved, and revered - in every heart, every home, every nation.

Let this be the prayer that shapes our lives: *"Father, may your name be honoured … in me … through me … around me … forevermore."*

4. 'YOUR KINGDOM COME'

Praying for a kingdom not of this world

Having begun The Lord's Prayer with reverence - *"Our Father in heaven, hallowed be your name"* - Jesus now leads us into the first grand petition that moves beyond adoration and into alignment: *"Your kingdom come."* (Matthew 6:10a).

These three words are profoundly simple and yet they are spiritually immense. This is not a vague or poetic phrase - it is a revolutionary cry. It is a bold prayer that calls for the invasion of God's reign into every space and structure of human existence.

When we pray, *"Your kingdom come,"* we are not asking God to take us away from earth to heaven - we are asking for heaven to come and invade the earth. This phrase is political, personal, prophetic, and deeply practical. It declares that God is King, and we want His rule to be established - in us, through us, and all around us. Let us now explore what it really means to pray, *"Your kingdom come."*

What is the kingdom of God?

To understand this petition, we must first ask: What is the kingdom of God? The phrase appears over 80 times in the New Testament, particularly in the teachings of Jesus. It is central to His ministry. From the beginning of His public proclamation, Jesus declared: *"The time has come. The kingdom of God has come near. Repent and believe the good news!"* (Mark 1:15)

The kingdom of God refers to God's sovereign rule - His reign over all creation. But in the ministry of Jesus, it also referred to the inbreaking of that reign into human history in a new and decisive way. In Jesus, the King had arrived. And with Him, the signs of the kingdom - healing, deliverance, forgiveness, and transformation.

So when we pray, *"Your kingdom come,"* we are asking for God's reign to be increasingly manifest - not only in the future, but now.

The 'now and not yet' of the kingdom

A really crucial concept in New Testament theology is that the kingdom of God has come, is coming, and will come.

> ➤ It has come through Jesus' life, death, and resurrection.
> ➤ It is coming as hearts are transformed, churches are planted, and the gospel spreads.
> ➤ It will come in fullness when Christ returns to reign over everything.

This means that when we pray, *"Your kingdom come,"* we are praying in three directions:

> ➤ Backward, in gratitude for the King who came.
> ➤ Presently, in longing for His rule to expand today.
> ➤ Forward, in hope for the day when His kingdom will be complete and eternal.

This threefold tension is what theologians call the *"now but not yet"* reality of the kingdom. We already experience the reign of God - in salvation, healing, justice, and peace. But we do not yet see its fullness. Evil still exists. Suffering continues. Injustice lingers. So we keep praying: *"Your kingdom come."*

A Prayer of allegiance

To pray *"Your kingdom come"* is not just making a request - it is a declaration of loyalty. Every kingdom has a king, and in this kingdom, that King is Jesus. So when we pray this line, we are renouncing every rival throne. We are rejecting the reign of self, of sin, of secularism, and of Satan. We are pledging allegiance to Christ. This makes The Lord's Prayer deeply political - not in a partisan way, but in the truest sense. We are declaring that God's reign is ultimate. Not the government's. Not the marketplace's. Not the culture's. Not even our own. In a world where so many powers compete for our loyalty - ideologies, parties, influencers, and desires - this prayer seriously reorients us. It says: *"Only one King deserves my life – now let His kingdom come."*

The kingdom is both personal and global

When we pray *"Your kingdom come,"* we are asking for God's rule to expand - and that expansion begins in our hearts. Before God can reign through us, He must reign in us. We cannot pray for the world to submit to Christ if we ourselves are resisting Him. So this prayer becomes intensely personal.

- ➤ Is He reigning over your decisions?
- ➤ Is He King in your relationships?
- ➤ Is He enthroned in your finances?
- ➤ Is His kingdom visible in how you respond to stress, temptation, and criticism?

Too often, we want God's kingdom to come to 'them' - to those people, those sinners, or those institutions. But Jesus invites us to start with ourselves. *"Let your kingdom come - in me Lord."* And yet this prayer doesn't stay personal. It then stretches outward - to our families, our churches, our whole communities, our cities, and to the ends of the earth. It's a missionary prayer. Therefore, when we say, *"Your kingdom come,"* we are praying for:

- ➤ The gospel to reach every unreached people group.
- ➤ Justice to roll on like a river.
- ➤ Righteousness to be established in society.
- ➤ Peace to rule in divided lands.
- ➤ Revival to awaken hearts near and far.

What God's kingdom looks like

What does this kingdom look like when it comes? Thankfully, Jesus showed us. His life and teaching painted a vivid picture of kingdom values. In the wonderful Beatitudes (Matthew 5:3–10), He described the citizens of His kingdom:

- ➤ The poor in spirit
- ➤ Those who mourn
- ➤ The meek
- ➤ The merciful

> ➤ The pure in heart
> ➤ The peacemakers
> ➤ The persecuted

In other words, the kingdom of God doesn't look like worldly power, fame, or dominance. It looks like humility, holiness, and love.

When Jesus healed the sick, forgave sinners, fed the hungry, and welcomed the outcast, He was showing us what the kingdom looks like in action. It's where the broken are restored, the proud are humbled, and the least become the greatest. So, when we pray, *"Your kingdom come,"* we are asking God to reproduce that kingdom life in our world - and in us. *"Your kingdom come"* is not a passive phrase. This is not wishful thinking. It is a powerful, courageous cry that refuses to accept the brokenness of this world as final.

It is the prayer of those who believe that God has more - more justice, more mercy, more healing, more life. It is the declaration of citizens who belong to another realm - who live under a different King, with a different agenda, and for a different glory. So we pray boldly, urgently, and daily: Your kingdom come.

The clash of kingdoms

When we pray *"Your kingdom come,"* we are declaring war - not with weapons or violence, but with truth, grace, and love. This truly is a spiritual battle. Because wherever God's kingdom advances, the kingdom of darkness resists. This world is already under the sway of another dominion. In 2 Corinthians 4:4, Paul described Satan as: *"The god of this age [who] has blinded the minds of unbelievers."* And John writes: *"The whole world is under the control of the evil one."* (1 John 5:19).

These verses remind us that we are not praying for God to tweak the status quo - we are praying for a radical overthrow of the present darkness. We are asking for the rule of God to invade enemy-occupied territory.

This is not a comfortable prayer. It's a dangerous one. It threatens the idols of culture, the systems of oppression, the apathy in the church, and the rebellion in our hearts. When we pray *"Your kingdom come,"* we are inviting disruption - divine disruption. Jesus Himself said in Matthew 10:34: *"Do not suppose that I have come to bring peace to the earth. I did not come to bring peace, but a sword."* He meant that His kingdom would create conflict - not because He delights in division, but because the truth will always be opposed by lies.

The kingdom and the Church

Some mistakenly think the church is the kingdom. That's not correct. The church is not the kingdom - but it is the instrument through which the kingdom advances. Jesus said: *"I will build my church, and the gates of Hades will not overcome it."* (Matthew 16:18). And just before His ascension, He said to His disciples: *"You will receive power when the Holy Spirit comes on you; and you will be my witnesses... to the ends of the earth."* (Acts 1:8)

The church is the community of the kingdom – it's the gathered people of God who live under the reign of Christ and carry His mission into the world. We are the 'embassy' of the kingdom of God in every generation and every nation. When we pray *"Your kingdom come,"* we are praying for the church to be renewed, empowered, and always faithful - not inward-looking or culture-conforming, but bold, holy, and fruitful. This means that revival in the church and the advancement of God's kingdom go hand in hand. We cannot expect the world to reflect God's reign if the church does not.

The kingdom comes through surrender

We often think the kingdom comes through activity - preaching, mission, justice, and service. And yes, those are all vital. But at its core, the kingdom of God advances through surrender. Jesus never said, *"Go and build the kingdom."* He said, *"Seek first his kingdom."* (Matthew 6:33). The kingdom is not built by human hands. It is received by those who humble themselves and align their hearts with the King.

It comes to the poor in spirit, the repentant, the obedient, and the surrendered. This is why The Lord's Prayer moves us from *"Hallowed be your name"* to *"Your kingdom come"* and then it moves immediately to *"Your will be done."* The kingdom comes where the King's will is done.

We can only truly pray *"Your kingdom come"* when we are willing to say, *"My kingdom go."* That means releasing our grip on control, comfort, and convenience. It means praying with open hands: *"Lord, rule in me - in my plans, my career, my relationships, my resources, my future."* This is not a weak posture. It is the posture of power - because God's kingdom moves through those who have laid down their own.

Praying for the kingdom in the everyday

The beauty of this petition is that it is not only grand - it is intensely practical. To pray *"Your kingdom come"* is not just to ask for global revival or Christ's return - it's also to invite His rule into every part of our daily lives. For example:

➢ When you choose forgiveness over bitterness - you are praying *"Your kingdom come."*
➢ When you speak truth in love - you are praying *"Your kingdom come."*
➢ When you serve without expecting recognition - you are praying *"Your kingdom come."*
➢ When you give generously to the poor - you are praying *"Your kingdom come."*
➢ When you raise children to know and love Jesus - you are praying *"Your kingdom come."*
➢ When you resist temptation and walk in holiness - you are praying *"Your kingdom come."*

This is where the kingdom advances - not only in pulpits and crusades, but in our kitchens, our classrooms, cafes, hospitals, workplaces, and neighbourhoods. Every act of faithfulness becomes an outpost of heaven.

The King we serve

Finally, this prayer points us to the heart of the King Himself. Jesus is not only the one who taught us to pray this way - He is the one who embodied the kingdom. Wherever Jesus went, the kingdom came with Him.

> ➢ He healed the sick - because the kingdom is about restoration.
> ➢ He forgave sinners - because the kingdom is about mercy.
> ➢ He fed the hungry - because the kingdom is about provision.
> ➢ He touched lepers - because the kingdom is about compassion.
> ➢ He confronted the religious elite - because the kingdom is about truth and justice.

Then at the cross, He wore a crown of thorns and was mocked as *"King of the Jews"* - yet through His suffering, He was enthroned as the true King of kings. His resurrection announced to the world that the kingdom of God had triumphed over death. So when we pray *"Your kingdom come,"* we are not praying to a far-off monarch. We are praying to the risen Jesus - the reigning King who is with us, for us, and returning in glory.

To pray *"Your kingdom come"* is to invite the rule of Jesus into every dimension of life - spiritual, moral, personal, social, and global. It is to live in alignment with His reign and to long for its fullness. This is a prayer of revolution, of surrender, of alignment, and of hope. Let it be our daily prayer - not only with our lips, but with our lives.

Longing for the fullness of the Kingdom

While the kingdom of God has broken into history through Jesus, it has not yet come in its fullness. Evil still exists. Injustice still prevails. Pain still touches every life. This is why we keep praying, *"Your kingdom come."* It is not only a prayer for God's reign now - it is a cry for His ultimate reign forever.

Paul speaks of this final fulfillment in 1 Corinthians 15:24-25: *"Then the end will come, when he hands over the kingdom to God the Father after he has destroyed all dominion, authority and power. For he must reign until he has put all his enemies under his feet."*

This is our hope: one day, Jesus will return to judge the living and the dead, to renew creation, to wipe away every tear, and to bring perfect justice and peace. This is the consummation of the kingdom - the day when what we pray for will be fully seen and fully experienced.

So when we say, *"Your kingdom come,"* we are not only aligning ourselves with God's purposes today; we are also expressing our longing for that glorious day to come. Revelation 11:15 declares: *"The kingdom of the world has become the kingdom of our Lord and of his Messiah, and he will reign for ever and ever."* This is the end of the story - and it's breathtaking. Every time we pray this line, we lean forward in anticipation.

But what do we do while we wait?

We live as citizens of that kingdom - right now. Paul writes: *"Our citizenship is in heaven. And we eagerly await a Saviour from there, the Lord Jesus Christ."* (Philippians 3:20). Even though we live in earthly nations, carry around earthly passports, and face earthly challenges, our true identity is rooted in this heavenly kingdom. This affects everything.

- ➢ We live by a different ethic.
- ➢ We are shaped by different values.
- ➢ We pursue different goals.
- ➢ We invest in different treasures.

While the world chases power, we serve. While the world seeks revenge, we forgive. While the world lives for now, we live for eternity. This kingdom life is not always easy. It often involves suffering and sacrifice. But it is marked by deep, unshakable hope. Because we know how the story ends. We know that our King is coming.

So we wait - not passively, but actively. We work for justice, preach the gospel, feed the hungry, plant churches, raise godly children, and make disciples. Every act of obedience is a small advance of the kingdom of God.

Opposition to the kingdom today

As the kingdom of God advances, it will always meet resistance. Jesus warned us of this. In Matthew 24:9, He said: *"You will be handed over to be persecuted and put to death, and you will be hated by all nations because of me."*

Throughout history, followers of Jesus have suffered for the sake of the kingdom - and many still do today. In some places, it's the loss of rights or freedoms. In others, it's imprisonment or martyrdom. And even in nations where there is no physical threat, believers often face mockery, isolation, or pressure to compromise.

Why? Because the kingdom of God always confronts the kingdoms of man. It challenges injustice. It exposes sin. It demands surrender. But take heart. Jesus also said in John 16:33, *"In this world you will have trouble. But take heart! I have overcome the world."* This is the confidence we carry when we pray, *"Your kingdom come."* We are not praying to some weak King. We are praying to the risen, reigning, returning Lord - and His kingdom cannot fail.

Becoming people of the kingdom

To pray this prayer is to become a certain kind of person - a kingdom person. What does that look like?

➤ It looks like Jesus: His life is the perfect picture of kingdom living - full of grace and truth, full of courage and compassion.
➤ It looks like the early church: A community of generosity, boldness, worship, and witness.
➤ It looks like holiness: Not a private morality, but a public testimony - a life set apart for God.

➢ It looks like faithfulness in ordinary life: Doing your work with excellence. Loving your spouse sacrificially. Raising your children in the fear of the Lord. Serving your neighbour without expecting praise. Forgiving even when it hurts so much.

Kingdom people don't wait for ideal circumstances. They live kingdom lives now - wherever God has placed them. You don't have to be a preacher, missionary, or theologian to live this way. You just have to belong to the King - and be willing to let Him reign in every area of your life.

Letting this prayer shape our desires

Finally, let's remember that prayer is not only a means of asking - it is a means of reshaping. When we pray, *"Your kingdom come,"* we are asking God to reorder our priorities and passion. We are asking Him to lift our eyes from selfish ambition to eternal purpose. Too often, our prayers revolve around comfort, success, safety, or outcomes we can control. But Jesus teaches us to start with something greater - God's reign. This prayer changes us.

➢ It challenges our consumerism.
➢ It convicts our complacency.
➢ It redirects our ambition.
➢ It reignites our hope.

And as it reshapes our hearts, it reshapes our world.

Conclusion

"Your kingdom come." Three small words - but they carry the weight of eternity. They are a cry of surrender, a call to mission, a longing for justice, and a declaration of hope. Every time we pray them, we are joining the prayer of saints and martyrs, of missionaries and mothers, of persecuted believers and faithful pastors, of children and elders, of the church throughout the ages. We are lifting our voices in unison with heaven and saying: *"Father, let your reign come in me, through me, around me, and soon - forevermore."* Until that day when the King returns and all things are made new, let this be our daily prayer: *"Your kingdom come."*

5. 'YOUR WILL BE DONE'

The boldest prayer of all

After praying *"Our Father in heaven, hallowed be your name. Your kingdom come,"* Jesus teaches us to say: *"Your will be done."* (Matthew 6:10b). This is perhaps the most daring and difficult prayer any believer can pray. While *"Your kingdom come"* calls for God's reign to spread, *"Your will be done"* demands a personal surrender from us - the kind of surrender that resists our natural inclination to assert our own plans, preferences, and desires.

These words are not passive. They are not resignation to fate. They are an act of deep trust – a brave declaration that God's will is better than ours, wiser than ours, and higher than ours, even when we don't understand it. This is the prayer of Gethsemane. It is the heartbeat of true discipleship. And it is a daily invitation to lay down our own rule and embrace the will of God - not just in theory, but in every part of life.

What do we mean by "God's will"?

Scripture speaks of God's will in several ways. For clarity, let's consider three dimensions:

A. God's Sovereign Will (What He Ordains)

    This refers to God's ultimate plan, which will happen no matter what. It includes His control over history, His purposes in creation, and His timing in redemption. Nothing can stop or alter this will. *"The Lord Almighty has sworn, 'Surely, as I have planned, so it will be, and as I have purposed, so it will happen.'"* (Isaiah 14:24)

B. God's Moral Will (What He Commands)

    This refers to how God desires His people to live - the principles revealed in Scripture: love, justice, mercy, faithfulness, humility. God's moral will is clearly expressed, but it can be disobeyed. *"Be joyful always; pray continually; give thanks in all circumstances, for this is God's will for you in Christ Jesus."* (1 Thessalonians 5:16–18)

C. God's Personal Will (What He Directs)

This refers to God's specific guidance in individual lives - whom to marry, where to live, what job to take, how to serve. This will is discerned through prayer, wisdom, counsel, and the leading of the Holy Spirit. When we pray, *"Your will be done,"* we are aligning ourselves with all these aspects of God's will - desiring His sovereign plan to unfold, His moral will to be obeyed, and His personal leading to be trusted.

The heart posture behind the prayer

Praying *"Your will be done"* is not merely asking God to override human decisions with divine power. It is asking Him to change our hearts so that we want what He wants. It's the opposite of the world's message, which constantly tells us: *"Follow your heart. Do what feels right. Be true to yourself."* But Scripture says: *"The heart is deceitful above all things and beyond cure. Who can understand it?"* (Jeremiah 17:9). So rather than trusting our own instincts, we come to God with open hands, saying, *"Father, lead me. Shape my desires. Direct my steps. Bend my will to yours."*

This is not a weak or passive posture - it is actually the strongest thing we can do. Because surrender to God's will requires faith, humility, and courage. It means trusting that God sees what we cannot see, knows what we cannot know, and loves us more than we love ourselves.

Jesus: The model of surrendered prayer

Nowhere is this prayer more powerfully illustrated than in the life of Jesus Himself. In the Garden of Gethsemane, just before His arrest, Jesus knelt and prayed: *"My Father, if it is possible, may this cup be taken from me. Yet not as I will, but as you will."* (Matthew 26:39). This is the deepest expression of what it means to pray, *"Your will be done."*

Jesus, in His humanity, felt the huge weight of what was coming - betrayal, torture, the burden of sin, and the agony of the cross. He asked His Father if there was another way. But ultimately, He surrendered.

His obedience wasn't mechanical - it was costly. He chose the Father's will over His personal comfort, reputation, and even survival. And through that surrender, the greatest act of redemption in history was accomplished. Every time we pray, *"Your will be done,"* we are walking the path that Jesus walked. We are echoing His prayer. And we are trusting that God's purposes, though sometimes painful, are always good.

The struggle of surrender

Let's be totally honest - this is not easy. We like control. We like predictability. We like our plans. Even when we say, *"Your will be done,"* part of us quietly hopes that God's will happens to align with our desires. But true prayer is not about getting our way. It is about God getting His way - in us and through us. This will then require of us: a continual laying down of pride; a continual resistance of the urge to manipulate circumstances; a continual choosing to believe that God's way is best, even when it seems hard, slow, or confusing. Surrender is not a one-time event - it's a whole lifestyle.

- ➤ It's surrendering our careers.
- ➤ It's surrendering our marriages.
- ➤ It's surrendering our dreams.
- ➤ It's surrendering our children.
- ➤ It's surrendering our timelines.
- ➤ It's surrendering our very selves.

Romans 12:1 calls us to this daily life of submission: *"Therefore, I urge you, brothers and sisters, in view of God's mercy, to offer your bodies as a living sacrifice, holy and pleasing to God - this is your true and proper worship."* This is precisely what it means to say, *"Your will be done."*

Aligning our prayers with God's will

This petition also teaches us how to pray. All too often, our prayers are a list of requests - for health, provision, protection, opportunity, and God invites us to bring those requests.

But those petitions must always be wrapped in surrender: *"Lord, this is what I hope for - but I trust you. Let your will be done."* This brings peace. Because once we've placed something in God's hands, we can rest. We don't need to anxiously control outcomes or manipulate people. We've handed it over to the One who knows best and will always do what's best.

This is the kind of prayer that the apostle John described in his first letter: *"This is the confidence we have in approaching God: that if we ask anything according to his will, he hears us."* (1 John 5:14). The more we know God's Word and walk with His Spirit, the more our hearts become aligned with His will - and the more our prayers reflect His purposes.

"Your will be done" is not a phrase of resignation - it is a bold declaration of ultimate trust. It is the cry of a child who believes their Father knows best. It is the song of a servant who finds joy in their Master's plan. It is the life posture of one who longs not just for answers, but for alignment. When we pray these words, we are stepping into the very heart of discipleship. We are saying: *"Father, rule in me. Reign over me. And lead me in the path of your will - whatever that may cost."* And that is where true peace and power are always found.

God's will in the big and the small

One of the great misconceptions about God's will is that it only applies to life's big decisions - who to marry, what job to take, where to live, which ministry to pursue. But Scripture presents a much broader - and more intimate - view of God's will. Paul writes in 1 Thessalonians 4:3, *"It is God's will that you should be sanctified."* In other words, God's will is not only about where you go or what you do - it's about who you are becoming.

When we pray *"Your will be done,"* we are not only seeking guidance for major crossroads. We are inviting the will of God to shape our daily lives - our thoughts, our habits, our relationships, our attitudes. Too often we want God to show us His will in the future, while He is inviting us to obey His will today.

➢ It is God's will that we speak truth, even when lying is easier.
➢ It is God's will that we forgive, even when revenge feels justified.
➢ It is God's will that we love our enemies, give to the needy, remain sexually pure, honour our commitments, and bear fruit that glorifies Him.

Discerning God's will in a noisy world

Praying for God's will is one thing. Discerning it is another - especially in a world filled with competing voices. How do we know what God's will is when it isn't specifically spelled out in Scripture?

Paul gives us a powerful principle in Romans 12:2: *"Do not conform to the pattern of this world but be transformed by the renewing of your mind. Then you will be able to test and approve what God's will is - his good, pleasing and perfect will."*

The key to discerning God's will is transformation. As our minds are renewed by the Word of God and shaped by the Spirit of God, we gain the ability to test and approve what aligns with God's heart. This happens through:

➢ *Scripture* - The primary way God reveals His will.
➢ *Prayer* - Communion with God tunes our hearts to His voice.
➢ *Wise counsel* - God speaks through the godly wisdom of others.
➢ *Providence* - Open and closed doors often signal divine leading.
➢ *Peace* - The Spirit often confirms God's will with settled conviction.

Discerning God's will is less about deciphering a blueprint and more about walking in step with the Spirit, trusting that He will lead as we follow in obedience.

When God's will is different than our will

Let's be honest: sometimes God's will is not what we want.

➤ We pray for healing, and the illness remains.

➤ We pray for a door to open, and it stays shut.

➤ We long for reconciliation, but the relationship ends.

➤ We plan for success, but failure comes instead.

In those moments, praying *"Your will be done"* is not easy - it's agonising. And yet, this is where the most powerful faith is formed. Faith that doesn't rely on outcomes, but on the character of the One Who holds the outcomes in His hand. We see this in the lives of biblical saints:

➤ **Joseph** suffered betrayal, slavery, and imprisonment. But later, he said to his brothers: *"You intended to harm me, but God intended it for good..."* (Genesis 50:20)

➤ **Job**, in the midst of unimaginable loss, declared: *"The Lord gave and the Lord has taken away; may the name of the Lord be praised."* (Job 1:21)

➤ **Paul**, when pleading for God to remove his *"thorn in the flesh,"* received this response: *"My grace is sufficient for you, for my power is made perfect in weakness."* (2 Corinthians 12:9)

These are not words of resignation. They are declarations of trust in the sovereignty and goodness of God - even when His will is painful, delayed, or unclear.

Trusting God's will in times of waiting

Waiting is one of the hardest aspects of walking in God's will. We know what we want. We know what we've prayed. We believe God is good. But He hasn't moved - yet.

And so we wait. In faith. In prayer. In trust. This is where we must remember that God's timing is just as perfect as His plan.

Isaiah 55:8-9 reminds us: *"'For my thoughts are not your thoughts, neither are your ways my ways,' declares the Lord. 'As the heavens are higher than the earth, so are my ways higher than your ways and my thoughts than your thoughts.'"* When we pray *"Your will be done,"* we are surrendering not just the what of God's plan, but the when. We are confessing that even delays are divine. That even silence has purpose. That even detours may be part of the destination.

It's in the waiting that our faith is refined. It's in the waiting that we learn patience, dependence, and perseverance. And it's in the waiting that we often encounter God most deeply.

Releasing control, embracing peace

At its very core, *"Your will be done"* is a prayer of release. It is the loosening of our white-knuckled grip on control. It is also the relinquishing of the illusion that we are in charge. It is also the peaceful surrender that comes from trusting in the wisdom, power, and love of God. This kind of surrender brings freedom.

➢ Freedom from anxiety - because God is in control.
➢ Freedom from striving - because we are led, not driven.
➢ Freedom from fear - because His will is always good.

Philippians 4:6–7 assures us: *"Do not be anxious about anything, but in every situation, by prayer and petition, with thanksgiving, present your requests to God. And the peace of God, which transcends all understanding, will guard your hearts and your minds in Christ Jesus."* This is the peace that comes not from getting our way, but from trusting in His.

When we say, *"Your will be done,"* we are choosing trust over anxiety, obedience over self-direction, and total surrender over stubbornness. We are opening the door for God's purposes to prevail - not just out there in the world, but right here in our hearts. It is a hard prayer, yes - but it is also a freeing one. Because it reminds us that we are not alone, not aimless, and not abandoned.

We have a Father in heaven, a Sovereign King, a good and gracious Shepherd Who leads us in paths of righteousness for His name's sake. And His will is not just better - it is perfect.

God's will on earth as it is in Heaven

Though part of the next phrase in The Lord's Prayer, the words *"on earth as it is in heaven"* also apply to *"Your will be done."* They define the scope and character of what we're asking. When we pray *"Your will be done on earth as it is in heaven,"* we are asking that the obedience, worship, and joy of heaven would invade this fallen world - and begin with us. In heaven, God's will is not questioned. It is not delayed. It is not debated. The angels always obey immediately, perfectly, and joyfully. Heaven operates in full harmony with God's will.

That is what we're asking for here on earth - in our families, our churches, our communities, and in our personal lives. Not half-hearted compliance, not reluctant surrender, but joyful, eager, reverent obedience that reflects heaven itself. This prayer brings heaven and earth together. It declares that we do not accept the brokenness of the world as permanent. It is a battle cry against sin, injustice, rebellion, and decay. It is the longing that God's perfect will would be done here - just as it is there.

Examples of faithful obedience in Scripture

Throughout the Bible, we see examples of people who embraced God's will, often at great personal cost - and in doing so, became part of His unfolding story.

➢ **Noah** obeyed God's command to build an ark despite years of ridicule and no visible sign of rain (Genesis 6-9).
➢ **Abraham** left his homeland not knowing where he was going, simply trusting the God who called him (Genesis 12).
➢ **Moses** returned to Egypt - the land he fled - to face Pharaoh and lead a nation to freedom (Exodus 3-4).
➢ **Esther** risked her life to stand before the king and save her people, declaring, *"If I perish, I perish"* (Esther 4:16).

➤ **Mary** responded to the angel's announcement with profound faith: *"I am the Lord's servant... May your word to me be fulfilled."* (Luke 1:38)

➤ **Jesus**, most of all, lived in perfect obedience to the Father - even to death on a cross (Philippians 2:8).

With the exception of Jesus, these men and women were not perfect, but they were all willing. And, like Jesus, through their surrender, God's will was done - on earth, as it is in heaven.

The cost and reward of obedience

Saying *"Your will be done"* is not always safe. In fact, it's rarely the easy road. But it is always the right one. Obedience may cost us popularity, comfort, or personal ambition. It may require that we step into situations that feel beyond us, foreign to us, or even frightening to us.

But obedience always leads us into deeper fellowship with God and greater fruit for His kingdom. As Jesus said in Matthew 16, *"Whoever wants to be my disciple must deny themselves and take up their cross and follow me."* (v.24). Yet Jesus also promised: *"Whoever loses their life for me will find it."* (v. 25).

That's the paradox of surrender. When we let go of our own will, we discover the joy and fullness of God's better will. The reward may not be comfort, but it will be communion. It may not be worldly success, but it will be eternal significance. And in the end, there is nothing greater than knowing we have walked in step with the purposes of God.

Praying "Your will be done" for others

It's important to recognise that this prayer is not only personal - it's also intercessory. We pray *"Your will be done"* not only for ourselves, but for others:

➤ *For friends who are lost* - that God's will for salvation would break through.

➢ *For churches that are divided* - that God's will for unity would be restored.

➢ *For nations in turmoil* - that God's will for justice and righteousness would be done.

➢ *For leaders in power* - that they would act according to God's truth.

➢ *For the persecuted Church* - that they would endure with faithfulness.

This kind of prayer reshapes how we view the world. Instead of reacting in fear, frustration, or despair, we pray with hope and confidence that God's will - not man's - will prevail.

As Paul wrote in 1 Timothy 2:1-4, we are to pray *"for all people,"* including kings and those in authority, because it is God's will that all people come to a knowledge of the truth. Intercessory prayer is one of the greatest ways we partner with God in seeing His will unfold on the earth.

Living a lifestyle of "Yes, Lord"

Ultimately, the prayer *"Your will be done"* must become more than just words - it must become a lifestyle. It must become the default setting of our hearts: *"Yes, Lord."*

➢ When a decision arises, we respond, *"Yes, Lord."*
➢ When a door opens - or closes - we say, *"Yes, Lord."*
➢ When His Word convicts us, we say, *"Yes, Lord."*
➢ When the path is unclear, we still say, *"Yes, Lord."*

This is the kind of heart God delights in. As Psalm 40:8 says: *"I desire to do your will, my God; your law is within my heart."* To pray *"Your will be done"* is to live each day open-handed and open-hearted, ready to obey, ready to trust, ready to follow.

This is not a one-time prayer - this is a day-by-day disposition. It is, in the truest sense, the heartbeat of Christian discipleship.

Conclusion

"Your will be done."

These four words, when prayed with sincerity, can change the trajectory of our lives. They express humility, trust, surrender, and worship. They align our hearts with heaven and anchor our feet on earth.

Jesus not only taught this prayer - He lived it. And now He calls us to do the same.

So may this be our prayer each morning, our anchor each night, and the theme of our lives: *"Not my will, Lord, but yours be done - in me, through me, and around me. On earth, as it is in heaven."*

6. 'ON EARTH AS IT IS IN HEAVEN'

Bridging heaven and earth

As we progress through The Lord's Prayer, we come to a phrase that ties the previous petitions together - *"on earth as it is in heaven."* (Matthew 6:10c). This line is more than a poetic flourish.

It is the heartbeat of the entire prayer. It reveals God's desire not to abandon earth for heaven, but to bring heaven's realities into earthly experience. It shows us that the Christian life is not about escape, but about engagement. Not about passively waiting for eternity, but about actively participating in God's redemptive purposes now.

When Jesus tells us to pray, *"on earth as it is in heaven,"* He is inviting us into a mission - to live in such a way that God's name is hallowed, His kingdom is visible, and His will is obeyed here and now, just as perfectly as it is in the realm of heaven.

Let's begin exploring what this powerful phrase means and how it shapes our faith, our worldview, and our daily living.

What is heaven really like?

To understand this prayer, we must first understand what Jesus meant by heaven. For many, the word evokes clouds, harps, angels, and a distant afterlife.

But the Bible gives a much richer picture. Heaven is the realm of God's immediate presence. It is where His authority is fully acknowledged; where His will perfectly is obeyed, and where His glory is unceasingly praised.

➢ In heaven, there is no sin - only holiness (Revelation 21:27).
➢ In heaven, there is no suffering - only joy (Revelation 21:4).
➢ In heaven, there is no rebellion - only worship (Isaiah 6:1-3).
➢ In heaven, God's will is not questioned - it is delighted in.

Heaven is not just a location. It is a reality - a dimension where God's purposes are fulfilled without resistance or delay. When we pray *"on earth as it is in heaven,"* we are asking for the values, character, and order of heaven to be manifested in our present world.

God's vision: heaven touching earth

From the beginning, God's plan has always been to dwell with His people - not just to reign from a distance. In Eden, heaven and earth were one. God walked with Adam and Eve in the cool of the day (Genesis 3:8). There was no separation between the divine and the human.

But sin fractured that unity, and ever since, God has been working to restore it. Throughout Scripture, we see glimpses of this amazing restoration:

➤ In the **tabernacle**, God dwelled among His people (Exodus 25:8).

➤ In the **temple**, His glory filled the Holy of Holies (1 Kings 8:10–11).

➤ In **Jesus**, 'God with us' became flesh and dwelt among us (John 1:14).

➤ In **the Church**, God's Spirit lives within us (1 Corinthians 6:19).

➤ And in **the new creation**, heaven and earth will be reunited forever (Revelation 21:1–3).

God's desire is not to rescue us from the earth, but to redeem the earth - to make it once again a place where His will is done and His presence is experienced. When we pray *"on earth as it is in heaven,"* we are agreeing with that vision.

An answer to the world's deepest longing

This petition is not only theological - it is profoundly personal and deeply global. We live in a world that longs for what heaven offers:

- ➢ Peace instead of war
- ➢ Justice instead of oppression
- ➢ Healing instead of disease
- ➢ Unity instead of division
- ➢ Love instead of hatred
- ➢ Light instead of darkness

Whether they know it or not, people everywhere ache for heaven's reality. They want what heaven embodies - wholeness, dignity, flourishing, beauty, and joy. And as believers, we carry that hope. Paul writes that even creation itself is waiting: *"The creation waits in eager expectation for the children of God to be revealed."* (Romans 8:19).

To pray *"on earth as it is in heaven"* is to long for the healing of the world, the renewal of all things, and the full restoration of God's good creation. It's a prayer for the mending of broken systems, broken communities, and broken hearts.

This is a missional prayer

When we say, *"on earth as it is in heaven,"* we are signing up for a mission. We are not just spectators hoping God will make the world better. We are His ambassadors (2 Corinthians 5:20), His workmanship (Ephesians 2:10), and we are also His sent ones - commissioned to be salt and light in the world. Jesus didn't just teach us to pray this prayer - He lived it. Everywhere He went, heaven touched earth:

- ➢ When He forgave sins, heaven came to the sinner.
- ➢ When He healed the sick, heaven came to the suffering.
- ➢ When He welcomed outcasts, heaven came to the marginalised.
- ➢ When He rebuked injustice, heaven came to the broken system.
- ➢ When He died and rose again, heaven came to all who believe.

Now He sends us to do the same - to live in such a way that when people encounter us, they encounter something of heaven. *"As the Father has sent me, I am sending you."* (John 20:21). So when we pray this line, we are not only longing for God to act - we are volunteering to participate. We are saying, *"Lord, use me. Let your will be done on earth - through my life."*

A prayer of hope in a world of hurt

Let's be honest here - some days it's hard to pray this prayer with confidence. We look around in the world and see chaos, conflict, and confusion. We see so many families torn apart, governments corrupted, the poor oppressed, the strong exploiting the weak. It can feel like heaven is far away. But this line of the Lord's Prayer is a hopeful protest against that brokenness. It says: *"This is not the way it's supposed to be. And it won't always be this way. God's kingdom is coming. His will is being done. And one day, all will be made right."* It is a prayer of resistance against despair. It is a cry of defiance against darkness. It is a bold declaration that heaven is not a fantasy - it is a promise. And the great news is, God has already begun fulfilling it in Christ.

"On earth as it is in heaven" is not a sentimental line tacked onto the end of a prayer. It is the very essence of what Jesus came to bring - the union of God's world and ours. When we pray these words, we are aligning with God's great redemptive plan. We are anchoring our hearts in hope. We are saying: *"Lord, let heaven touch earth - beginning with me."*

Living as agents of heaven on earth

When we pray *"on earth as it is in heaven,"* we are not only asking for divine intervention - we literally are offering ourselves as instruments. This phrase is not merely devotional - it is intensely practical. It calls us to live out heavenly realities in our earthly contexts. This is what Paul had in mind when he wrote: *"We are therefore Christ's ambassadors, as though God were making his appeal through us."* (2 Corinthians 5:20). As ambassadors of heaven, we represent the rule, culture, and priorities of the kingdom of God - wherever we are.

This therefore means:

- ➤ In a culture of greed, we practice generosity.
- ➤ In a culture of division, we live with reconciliation.
- ➤ In a culture of self-promotion, we serve in humility.
- ➤ In a culture of fear, we walk by faith.
- ➤ In a culture of relativism, we stand for truth in love.

To live as a heavenly citizen is to be noticeably different - not strange or obnoxious, but radiant. Like Daniel in Babylon. Like Joseph in Egypt. Like Esther in Persia. Like the early church in Rome. Heaven was visible in their lives - not because they shouted louder, but because they shone brighter. Jesus said: *"Let your light shine before others, that they may see your good deeds and glorify your Father in heaven."* (Matthew 5:16). That's what it looks like to live "on earth as it is in heaven."

Heaven-shaped worship and community

This petition also shapes the way we think about the church. The local church is not a social club or performance venue - it is a colony of heaven. It is that spiritual outpost where all the realities of God's kingdom are visible and tangible.

In Acts 2, the early church gave us a glimpse of heaven on earth: *"They devoted themselves to the apostles' teaching and to fellowship, to the breaking of bread and to prayer... They sold property and possessions to give to anyone who had need... And the Lord added to their number daily those who were being saved."* (Acts 2:42–47)

This was not just religious routine. It was a radical expression of heavenly values - selfless love, shared life, generosity, worship, and mission. It was a place where God's name was hallowed, His kingdom was expanding, and His will was being done - on earth, as it is in heaven. When we gather as believers - in buildings, in homes, in small groups or large - we are creating a space where heaven meets earth. Every act of hospitality, every prayer, every meal shared in Christ's name becomes an echo of the eternal reality of heaven.

Justice and mercy as kingdom priorities

Heaven is not only about worship; it is also about justice. God's throne is established on righteousness. His heart beats for the poor, the marginalised, the orphan, the widow, the refugee, the outcast. Psalm 89:14 tells us: *"Righteousness and justice are the foundation of your throne; love and faithfulness go before you."*

So if we are praying, *"on earth as it is in heaven,"* then we must care deeply about the things God cares about. That means engaging with injustice not as angry reactionaries, but as faithful kingdom citizens.

This requires:

➢ Speaking up for the voiceless.
➢ Serving the least and the last.
➢ Resisting systems of exploitation.
➢ Practising generosity, even when it costs us.
➢ Building communities that reflect God's concern for the vulnerable.

The prophet's words still ring true in Micah 6:8: *"He has shown you, O mortal, what is good. And what does the Lord require of you? To act justly and to love mercy and to walk humbly with your God."* Heaven is a place of justice, and the church is called to be a preview of that justice on earth.

Letting this prayer shape our homes

While this petition certainly applies globally, it also begins at home. Heaven on earth doesn't only mean missions, miracles, or movements. It means marriages shaped by grace; parenting shaped by patience; homes filled with forgiveness, prayer, joy and honour. Colossians 3 gives us a picture of this kind of living: *"Whatever you do, whether in word or deed, do it all in the name of the Lord Jesus..."* (v. 17). And then in verses 18–21: *"Wives, submit yourselves to your husbands; Husbands, love your wives and do not be harsh with them; Children, obey your parents; Fathers, do not embitter your children..."*

Heaven on earth is seen when spouses treat each other with Christlike love, when children are nurtured in the Lord, when peace and kindness fill our daily lives. So when we pray this line, we must also ask: Is God's will being done in my home - as it is in heaven? And if not, are we willing to be part of that change?

Heaven-driven prayer and mission

This line of The Lord's Prayer also renews our passion for prayer and mission. If we truly long for God's will to be done on earth as in heaven, then we will pray more fervently - and live more intentionally. We will pray for:

- ➤ The lost to be saved.
- ➤ The church to be revived.
- ➤ The nations to be reached.
- ➤ The suffering to be comforted.
- ➤ The darkness to be pushed back.

But we won't stop there. We will give, go, speak, serve, and build for the sake of the gospel - not to earn God's favour, but because we've already received it.

When Isaiah encountered the glory of God in heaven, he heard a voice asking, *"Whom shall I send?" His response was: "Here am I. Send me!"* (Isaiah 6:8). That must be our posture too. *"Father, let your will be done on earth, as it is in heaven - and let me be part of it."*

When we pray, *"on earth as it is in heaven,"* we are not escaping reality - we are actually engaging it. We are refusing to accept the brokenness of this world as final. We are embracing the call to live as salt and light, ambassadors and builders, worshippers and workers.

This is a prayer which always starts in our hearts, reshapes our homes, empowers the church, and overflows into every corner of society. And every time we pray it sincerely, heaven moves - because we are praying in alignment with God's own desire.

Anticipating the new heaven and new earth

As we pray *"on earth as it is in heaven,"* we are not only asking God to shape our present reality - we are expressing a deep and enduring hope for the future. This is a prayer anchored in the promise of complete renewal. It points forward to the day when heaven and earth will no longer be separate realms. The apostle John records this vision towards the end of the Bible:

"Then I saw 'a new heaven and a new earth,' for the first heaven and the first earth had passed away... And I heard a loud voice from the throne saying, 'Look! God's dwelling place is now among the people, and he will dwell with them. They will be his people, and God himself will be with them and be their God.' He will wipe every tear from their eyes. There will be no more death' or mourning or crying or pain, for the old order of things has passed away.'" (Revelation 21:1-4)

This is the ultimate fulfilment of The Lord's Prayer. The day is coming when God's name will be perfectly hallowed, His kingdom fully established, and His will eternally done - in every place and in every heart. Until then, our lives are shaped by that hope. We live in the *'now'* and the *'not yet.'* The kingdom has come, but not in its fullness. Our prayer, *"on earth as it is in heaven,"* is a cry for that final day, even as we work for glimpses of it in the here and now.

Hope that sustains us in suffering

This forward-looking hope is not escapist - it's empowering. It gives strength to persevere in trials and to labour in love, knowing that our efforts are not in vain.

Paul encouraged the church in Corinth with these words in 1 Corinthians 15:58 : *"Therefore, my dear brothers and sisters, stand firm. Let nothing move you. Always give yourselves fully to the work of the Lord, because you know that your labour in the Lord is not in vain."* Why is it not in vain? Because resurrection is coming. Because Christ is returning. Because heaven and earth will be made one, and every tear will be wiped away.

This hope fuels our endurance:

- ➤ It keeps us faithful when justice is slow.
- ➤ It keeps us praying when the answers are delayed.
- ➤ It keeps us joyful when the burdens are heavy.
- ➤ It keeps us pure when temptation is strong.

Our small acts of love, obedience, and sacrifice are seeds of the new creation. They are signposts that point to the day when Christ will make all things new.

The prayer that changes the one praying

Ultimately, this line of The Lord's Prayer changes not just the world around us - it changes us. When we consistently pray, *"on earth as it is in heaven,"* we begin to think more like citizens of heaven. Our values shift. Our priorities are reordered. Our hearts beat more in sync with God's.

- ➤ We become more *patient*, because we trust God's timing.
- ➤ We become more *courageous*, because we know the end of the story.
- ➤ We become more *generous*, because we're storing treasure in heaven.
- ➤ We become more *compassionate*, because we see people through God's eyes.

This is the great irony of prayer: we think we are asking God to act, and He is - but very often, He starts with us. He shapes our thoughts, redirects our desires, and empowers our obedience. The more we pray this prayer, the more we become the answer to it.

How do we begin living this prayer?

I delivered a whole teaching series on this one line in The Lord's Prayer and I wrote a book covering the same material. That would be the place to go for an in-depth answer to this question.

It's easy to be overwhelmed by the grand scope of "on earth as it is in heaven." But we must remember that this prayer begins in everyday life - in many small decisions, consistent obedience, and unseen faithfulness. Here are some places to start:

> *In your private life:* Does your prayer life reflect heaven's priorities? Are you seeking God's glory before your own comfort?

> *In your family:* Are you creating a home where grace, truth, and worship flourish?

> *In your work:* Are you treating people with dignity and excellence, working as unto the Lord?

> *In your neighbourhood:* Are you engaging the brokenness around you with compassion and presence?

> *In your church:* Are you contributing to a community where God's will is pursued and His love displayed?

The kingdom of heaven begins with mustard seeds - tiny acts that grow into something which is far beyond our control or comprehension. So don't despise small beginnings. Every time you love, serve, give, forgive, or speak truth - heaven is breaking into earth.

A preview of heaven

At its core, this line of the prayer is about manifestation - letting the reality of heaven break through into this world. And when the church truly lives this way, we become a preview of eternity. The watching world catches glimpses of something different:

> A love that doesn't give up.
> A joy that cannot be shaken.
> A unity that defies division.
> A holiness that shines in the dark.
> A peace that passes understanding.

This is what it means to be salt and light (Matthew 5:13–16). We're not here to condemn the world - we're here to show it what heaven looks like. And we do so not with arrogance, but with grace. Not shouting, but shining. Not with condemnation, but with compassion. Because we are not the destination - we are the signposts pointing to it.

Conclusion

"On earth as it is in heaven." This prayer is an invitation to dream with God. To align our hearts with His great mission. To participate in the renewal of all things. It's a dangerous prayer - because it calls us out of passivity and into participation. But it's also a hopeful prayer - because it assures us that heaven is not far off, and God is not finished with this world.

So let's keep praying it - with faith, with longing, with obedience: *"Father, let your kingdom come. Let your will be done. On earth - in my life, in my church, in my neighbourhood, in my nation - as it is in heaven."* And one day, when Christ returns and heaven and earth are one, we will rejoice to see that every whispered prayer, every quiet act of faithfulness, every tear and every triumph was not in vain.

The Lord's Prayer is not just a liturgy. It is a life. Let us live it - on earth, as it is in heaven.

7. 'GIVE US TODAY OUR DAILY BREAD'

From Heaven to the kitchen table

So far in The Lord's Prayer, our focus has been directed toward God: His name, His kingdom, His will. These are eternal, cosmic priorities. But with the fourth petition - *"Give us today our daily bread"* - the tone changes. The prayer moves from heaven to earth, from the throne of God to the kitchen table. Jesus now teaches us to bring our basic, physical needs before our heavenly Father. It is a stunning shift. The infinite God Who rules the cosmos also invites us to ask Him for something as simple and earthy as bread. That's how near, how loving, and how attentive our Father truly is. This one short line carries layers of meaning - about dependence, provision, contentment, community, and trust. In this chapter, we will begin exploring what it means to pray, *"Give us today our daily bread."*

A prayer of dependence

The first and most obvious we learn from this petition teaches is dependence. Jesus wants His followers to approach God as the source of all provision. Bread, in this context, represents the basic essentials of life - food, shelter, clothing, health, - everything needed to sustain us from day by day. It's so easy to forget how dependent we all actually are. Especially in developed nations, where supermarkets are stocked, pantries are full, and online delivery is a click away, we can begin to think of our daily provision as something we earn or control. But Jesus reminds us that everything we have comes from God.

James reminds us: *"Every good and perfect gift is from above, coming down from the Father of the heavenly lights, who does not change like shifting shadows."* (James 1:17). Whether we realise it or not, we are always living on grace. Every meal we eat, every breath we take, every beat of our hearts is sustained by God's kindness. This prayer re-orients our hearts - it reminds us that we are not self-sufficient. We are His creatures - and He is our Creator and our Provider.

The bread is "daily"

One of the most unique features of this verse is the term *"daily bread."* The Greek word used here is *'epiousios'* and it appears nowhere else in any ancient Greek literature. Many scholars have debated its meaning, but most agree it points to the bread we need for today – as opposed to a stockpile for the future.

This echoes the story of God providing manna in the wilderness. In Exodus 16, God told the Israelites to gather only enough manna for each day. If they tried to store it up, it would rot. The lesson was simple: trust God each day for the needs of that day.

In the same way, Jesus encourages us in Matthew 6:34 not to worry about tomorrow. He teaches us to live in daily trust. We are not to be consumed with future anxieties or self-preservation. Instead, we are to rest in God's faithfulness - one day at a time. This petition challenges our cultural addiction to accumulation.

In a world that glorifies abundance and savings and security, Jesus teaches us to live with open hands. It's not wrong to plan or prepare. But our confidence must rest not in what we have stored - but in the One Who never fails to provide.

This is a corporate prayer

Notice the wording: *"Give us today our daily bread."* This prayer is not in the singular. It's not *"Give me my bread."* It is our bread. This is a communal prayer. It reminds us that we are part of a body, a people, a family. When we ask God for daily bread, we are not just thinking of ourselves - we are lifting the needs of our neighbours and brothers and sisters before the Lord. This line in The Lord's Prayer should expand our compassion:

➢ When we see those who have no bread, we are moved to share ours.
➢ When we see global hunger, we are stirred to pray and act.
➢ When we see economic injustice, we are compelled to speak out and pursue change.

This is not a passive prayer. It invites generosity and justice. We cannot sincerely ask God to provide daily bread while ignoring the millions who go without it - especially if we are holding on to more than we need.

1 John 3:17-18 offers a sobering challenge: *"If anyone has material possessions and sees a brother or sister in need but has no pity on them, how can the love of God be in that person? Dear children, let us not love with words or speech but with actions and in truth."* Praying for our daily bread requires us to also be part of the answer - wherever we can.

God cares about physical needs

It's important to see the dignity Jesus gives to material needs. Sometimes we fall into the trap of thinking God only cares about our spiritual lives - our souls, our worship, our moral choices. But here, in the heart of the most famous prayer, Jesus tells us to ask for something as basic as bread. This affirms something profound: God cares about your body. He made it. He sustains it. He feeds it. And He will one day raise it in glory.

Too often, Christian teaching has fallen into dualism - the idea that the soul matters but the body doesn't. Jesus rejects that idea. He healed bodies. He fed people. He touched lepers. He ate with friends. And He rose from the dead in a real, physical body. So, when you are tired, hungry, sick, or struggling - you can come to God and ask for provision without shame. He is not only the God of the eternal - He is also the God of today. As Psalm 145:15-16 reminds us: *"The eyes of all look to you, and you give them their food at the proper time. You open your hand and satisfy the desires of every living thing."* Our Father's hand is open - we are invited to ask.

"Give us today our daily bread." This short petition teaches us to live in humble dependence, to trust God one day at a time, to carry one another in prayer, and to know that our physical needs matter to our heavenly Father. As we continue this study, we will see how this prayer calls each of us to a life of simplicity, gratitude, and deep faith - not in bread itself, but in the One Who provides it.

Bread and the character of God

When we pray, *"Give us today our daily bread,"* we are not merely requesting physical sustenance - we are anchoring ourselves in the nature and character of God. This line reminds us of who God is: our Father, our Provider, and our Sustainer. God is not reluctant to meet our needs. He is not stingy, distant, or forgetful. He is eager to provide for His children.

As Jesus later teaches in this same chapter of Matthew: *"Look at the birds of the air; they do not sow or reap or store away in barns, and yet your heavenly Father feeds them. Are you not much more valuable than they?"* (Matthew 6:26).

This petition helps recalibrate our view of God. Many people carry unconscious images of God as cold, demanding, or disinterested. But Jesus says clearly , *"No - He is your Father, and He delights in caring for you."* To ask for bread is to lean into God's goodness. It's to trust that He knows what we need, even before we ask Him (Matthew 6:8). It's to approach Him not as beggars, but as beloved children.

Bread and contentment

Embedded in this simple prayer is a very powerful invitation to contentment. We are asking for bread - not banquets, not luxury, not excess. Just bread. Just what we need for today. This challenges the endless consumerism of our age. The culture around us constantly urges us to want more - more possessions, more options, more comfort, more control. But Jesus teaches us to pray for enough. Not because God is unwilling to give more, but because true peace is found in sufficiency - not in surplus.

Proverbs 30:8-9 also echoes this very sentiment: *"Give me neither poverty nor riches but give me only my daily bread. Otherwise, I may have too much and disown you and say, 'Who is the Lord?' Or I may become poor and steal and so dishonour the name of my God."* There is great spiritual danger in both lack and abundance. But there is deep joy in daily provision. To pray for daily bread is to say, *"Lord, I don't need everything - just what you know I need today."*

Such a posture cultivates gratitude, humility, and freedom. It loosens our grip on material things. It reminds us that happiness is never found in accumulation, but always in God's faithful presence and provision.

Bread and the discipline of simplicity

This petition also leads us into the ancient Christian discipline of simplicity. Asking for daily bread encourages us to live lives that are uncluttered, unburdened by greed, and rooted in trust rather than anxiety. Simplicity is not about poverty - it's all about focus. It's about living with intention. It's about freeing ourselves from the tyranny of excess so we can focus more clearly on God's kingdom.

Jesus said in Luke 12:15: *"Watch out! Be on your guard against all kinds of greed; life does not consist in an abundance of possessions."* Simplicity is countercultural. It resists all the noise, speed, and consumerism of the modern world. It says, *"I will not be enslaved by more. I will be content with enough."*

This prayer trains our hearts in that direction. When we begin to delight in daily bread - when we stop demanding more - we begin to experience a peace that eludes those chasing constant increase. To live simply is to trust that God is enough. That He can be trusted with tomorrow. That He is the Bread of Life.

Bread and the Bread of Life

While this petition clearly refers to our material needs, it also points us to a deeper hunger - one that bread alone cannot satisfy. In John 6, after feeding the five thousand with literal bread, Jesus says: *"Very truly I tell you, it is not Moses who has given you the bread from heaven, but it is my Father who gives you the true bread from heaven. For the bread of God is the bread that comes down from heaven and gives life to the world."* (John 6:32–33).

And then He declares in John 6:35, *"I am the bread of life. Whoever comes to me will never go hungry, and whoever believes in me will never be thirsty."*

So, this petition - *"Give us today our daily bread"* - is not just about breakfast. It's about Jesus. He is our ultimate sustenance. He is our portion. He is the only food that truly satisfies the soul. To pray this line is to say, *"Lord God, meet my physical needs - but more than that, feed my spirit with the presence of your Son."* We are not simply asking for provision; we are seeking communion.

Gratitude for the ordinary

This prayer also teaches us to find wonder in the ordinary. Bread is not an extravagant request. It is common, every day, basic. And that's part of the beauty. God invites us to bring even our smallest needs before Him. He is not bothered by our daily concerns. On the contrary, He delights in providing for them. And when we receive these gifts - food, rest, friendship, warmth, work - we are called to receive them with joy and thanksgiving. Paul reminds us in 1 Timothy 4:4-5: *"For everything God created is good, and nothing is to be rejected if it is received with thanksgiving, because it is consecrated by the word of God and prayer."*

Gratitude transforms ordinary moments into sacred ones. A simple meal, received as a gift from God, becomes an act of worship. When we slow down and say, *"Thank you, Lord, for today's bread,"* we begin to see God's fingerprints everywhere. This is the life Jesus invites us into - not constant striving for what we lack, but deep joy in what we've been given. The prayer for daily bread invites us into a different way of living - one marked by trust, contentment, simplicity, and gratitude. It reminds us that God is not only concerned with our eternity, but also with our daily reality. Every time we pray these words, we are resisting the anxiety of a world that says, *"You don't have enough,"* and embracing the peace of a Father who says, *"I am enough."* So we pray, not with fear, but with confidence: *"Give us today our daily bread."*

Bread and generosity

As we pray "Give us today our daily bread," and receive from God's hand all that we need, we are called to live generously. This petition is not about hoarding but about sharing.

It's about remembering that what we receive is not just for us - it's also for others. Paul writes in 2 Corinthians 9:10-11: *"Now he who supplies seed to the sower and bread for food will also supply and increase your store of seed and will enlarge the harvest of your righteousness. You will be enriched in every way so that you can be generous on every occasion, and through us your generosity will result in thanksgiving to God."* We are blessed in order to be a blessing. When we pray for daily bread and God provides, we must ask: Is there someone near me who needs part of this provision?

In Acts 4:32-35, the early church lived this out in radical ways. No one claimed personal ownership of their possessions. They shared everything freely. There were no needy persons among them - not because everyone had the same income, but because everyone had the same heart. To live with this kind of open-handed generosity is to embody the kingdom of God. It's not charity - it's worship. It's not mere philanthropy - it's obedience to the God Who gave us our daily bread and now invites us to pass it along.

Bread and justice

This petition also reminds us that not everyone has daily bread - and that is not God's design. While God provides, the systems and structures of this fallen world often block access to His provision for many people. This means that praying *"Give us today our daily bread"* is not just a personal request. It is also a cry for justice - that all people might receive what God intends for them. We must not become numb to the suffering of those who go without - whether they are in distant nations or our own communities. When we see children malnourished, families displaced, or elderly neighbours who are living in poverty, this prayer must stir our hearts to action.

Isaiah 58:6-7 offers God's heart for justice: *"Is not this the kind of fasting I have chosen: to loose the chains of injustice and untie the cords of the yoke, to set the oppressed free and break every yoke? Is it not to share your food with the hungry and to provide the poor wanderer with shelter - when you see the naked, to clothe them, and not to turn away from your own flesh and blood?"*

To pray for daily bread is to join God's mission of restoration - to be people who speak, serve, and advocate for the vulnerable. It's about building a world where everyone has enough.

Bread, sabbath, and rest

There's another often-overlooked layer to this petition: it invites us into rhythms of rest. In Exodus 16, when God gave manna in the wilderness, He instructed Israel to collect twice as much on the sixth day and to rest on the seventh. No manna fell on the Sabbath. Why? Because God wanted His people to learn to trust and rest. To know that they could pause from striving and still be sustained by Him.

When we pray for daily bread, we are also declaring, *"I don't need to live in constant hustle. I can pause. I can Sabbath. I can rest. I can breathe."* In a world of busyness, this is a radical act of faith. It's a refusal to be defined by productivity. It's a reminder that we are not machines - we are children of a generous Father who gives us what we need even while we rest.

Bread and worship

Receiving bread from God - daily - should inspire worship. Each time we eat, each time we see His hand of provision, we are reminded of His goodness and faithfulness. Deuteronomy 8:10 commands: *"When you have eaten and are satisfied, praise the Lord your God for the good land he has given you."*

We live in an age of ingratitude. But this prayer reawakens us to God's constant care. It trains us to see each meal as a miracle, each provision as a gift.

Meals should become moments of praise. Grace before meals should not be a rushed ritual, but a joyful declaration: *"Lord, you have provided again. Thank you."* When Jesus broke bread with His disciples, He gave thanks. When He fed the five thousand, He looked up to heaven and gave thanks. Gratitude was always part of His rhythm - and it should be part of ours.

Bread, communion, and Christ

The most profound layer of this prayer is how it points us to the table of the Lord - the place where bread becomes more than bread. At the Last Supper, Jesus took bread, gave thanks, broke it, and gave it to His disciples, saying: *"Take and eat; this is my body."* (Matthew 26:26)

This is the bread we need most - the bread of salvation. When we receive communion, we are being reminded that Christ is the true Bread of Life. He is our sustenance, our satisfaction, and our strength. So even as we pray for physical nourishment, we are also reminded of the spiritual feast set before us. Every time we receive the bread of communion, we remember: God has already given us the greatest provision of all - Himself.

"Give" is a word of grace

Finally, consider the first word of the petition: *"Give."* We are not demanding. We are not purchasing. We are not earning. We are asking. This is the posture of grace. Everything we receive from God - including daily bread - is a gift. We don't deserve it. We don't control it. We simply open our hands in trust and say, *"Father, give."* And He does just that - again and again. Faithfully. Patiently. Lovingly. This prayer humbles us. It reminds us that we live not by entitlement, but by mercy. We are not masters of our fate - we are children of grace.

Conclusion

"Give us today our daily bread." It is a short line, but it holds the weight of heaven. It draws our eyes to a faithful Father, our hands to generosity, our hearts to worship, and our lives to trust. This petition anchors us in the now. It trains us to live in the present, to walk by faith, to delight in God's goodness, and to share with others what we receive. So may we pray this daily. May we live this honestly. And may we never forget the Giver - the One Who not only gives bread but gave Himself for us.

8. 'FORGIVE US OUR SINS'

The heartbeat of the Gospel

If *"Give us today our daily bread"* addresses our physical need, then *"Forgive us our sins"* addresses our deepest spiritual need. It brings us to the heart of the gospel - the truth that we are sinners in need of mercy, and that God, through Jesus Christ, freely forgives. This petition is more than a request. It's a confession, a cry for grace, and an invitation into the rhythm of mercy. Here, Jesus teaches us not only to seek forgiveness but to live as people shaped by it - offering the same grace to others that we ourselves have received.

The necessity of forgiveness

Before we can pray this line sincerely, we must come to terms with a simple but often resisted truth: we need forgiveness. Romans 3:23 states: *"For all have sinned and fall short of the glory of God."* Sin is not just breaking rules - it's rebellion against the heart and will of God. It's choosing our way over His, whether through pride, deceit, lust, greed, or neglect. It infects both our actions and our intentions.

We often like to think of ourselves as *"good people who sometimes make mistakes."* But Scripture tells us that sin is deeper than error - it is a condition. And the only remedy is the mercy of God. To ask God to forgive us is to humbly admit that we have fallen far short - and that we simply cannot fix ourselves. This is a deeply countercultural truth in a world that always seems to prize self-sufficiency and moral relativism.

God's desire to forgive

But just as we must see the truth of our sin, we must also see the greater truth of God's mercy. Psalm 86:5 says: *"You, Lord, are forgiving and good, abounding in love to all who call to you."* This is Who God is - not a reluctant judge but a compassionate Father, eager to pardon. Throughout Scripture, God reveals Himself as the One Who forgives sin, cleanses guilt and removes our transgressions *"as far as the east is from the west."* (Psalm 103:12).

Forgiveness is not something God offers begrudgingly - it flows from His very character. This is why Jesus could tell stories like the parable of the prodigal son (Luke 15), where the father runs to embrace the returning rebel. That's the kind of God we pray to when we say, *"Forgive us our sins."*

Forgiveness through Christ

Of course, God's forgiveness is not arbitrary - it is costly. It flows to us through the blood of Jesus Christ. The Apostle Paul tells us: *"In him we have redemption through his blood, the forgiveness of sins, in accordance with the riches of God's grace."* (Ephesians 1:7). The cross is the foundation of our forgiveness. Jesus bore the weight of our sin. He paid the debt we could never repay. When we ask for forgiveness, we are not hoping that God might overlook our sin - we are standing on the finished work of Christ, who has already dealt with it. This is why forgiveness is both free and serious. Free - because it's a gift of grace. Serious - because it cost Jesus everything.

Confession and repentance

This petition also teaches us that our experience of forgiveness and confession are linked. We must name our sins before God - not to inform Him (He already knows), but to align our hearts with truth. 1 John 1:9 assures us: *"If we confess our sins, he is faithful and just and will forgive us our sins and purify us from all unrighteousness."* Confession is not about wallowing in shame - it's about stepping into the light. It's the doorway to healing and restoration. True confession also moves us into repentance - a turning away from sin and toward God. When we say, *"Forgive us our sins,"* we are not merely asking for a clean slate. We already have that, in Christ. We are expressing our desire to be changed - to walk in newness of life. We are asking that the power of forgiveness would change our attitudes and actions.

Daily forgiveness for daily sin

It's important to note that Jesus places this petition in a daily prayer. Just as we ask for daily bread, we ask for daily grace. This doesn't mean we are constantly being re-saved - but it does mean we need continual renewal in our relationship with God.

Even as believers, we stumble. We fail. We forget who we are. We forget that we are already forgiven and we can easily take that for granted. And so we return - daily - to the fountain of mercy. Not to earn God's love and grace and forgiveness, but to experience it afresh.

Jesus illustrated this beautifully when He washed His disciples' feet in John 13. Peter, at first, resisted. But Jesus said: *"Unless I wash you, you have no part with me."* (John 13:8). And then He clarified: *"Those who have had a bath need only to wash their feet; their whole body is clean."* (John 13:10). In other words: you've been made clean, but you still need your feet washed. We come to God daily with dusty feet, and He kneels, tenderly, to cleanse us again.

When we pray, *"Forgive us our sins,"* we are not grovelling before a hard-hearted deity who hasn't forgiven us. We are returning to the One Who ran to meet the prodigal. We are opening ourselves to the grace that flows from the cross. We are being restored - not just to innocence, but to intimacy with God. This is the gospel in prayer form: we are sinners, and God is merciful. We are broken, and He is the Healer. We fall short, and He lifts us up.

Forgiven people forgive people

The second half of this petition - *"as we forgive those who sin against us"* - is one of the most sobering and challenging lines in The Lord's Prayer. It ties God's forgiveness of us to our forgiveness of others. Jesus connects the mercy we receive from God to the mercy we give to others. At first glance, this seems transactional - as though God will only forgive us if we forgive others. But Jesus is not introducing a condition that earns forgiveness. That would completely undo the whole reality of salvation by grace, through faith. Rather, He is describing the natural outworking of a heart that has truly experienced grace. He is talking about the impact and effect of forgiveness and unforgiveness. Those who know the weight of their own sin, and the wonder of their pardon, cannot help but extend forgiveness to others. It's not always easy. But it's always possible through the Holy Spirit.

Remarkably, this is the only line in The Lord's Prayer that Jesus returns to and immediately expands upon after the prayer ends. In Matthew 6:14-15, He says: *"For if you forgive other people when they sin against you, your heavenly Father will also forgive you. But if you do not forgive others their sins, your Father will not forgive your sins."* Why does Jesus highlight this point so strongly? Because He knows how easily unforgiveness can poison the soul. Nothing blocks the effect and experience of grace in our lives like bitterness and forgiveness.

When we withhold forgiveness, we cut across the impact of the grace which God has lavished upon us in Christ. We don't stop His grace, for it has already been given, once and for all, but we certainly stop its impact in our lives when we refuse to forgive. We may think we are punishing the offender - but we are the ones who become imprisoned. Jesus is clear: forgiveness is not optional for those who follow Him.

What forgiveness is - and what it is not

To obey this command, we need a clear understanding of what forgiveness actually means.

Forgiveness is:

➢ Releasing someone from the debt they owe you.
➢ Choosing to entrust justice to God.
➢ Letting go of resentment and the right to revenge.
➢ A decision - often repeated over time - to walk in grace.

Forgiveness is not:

➢ Excusing or minimizing the offence.
➢ Pretending the hurt didn't happen.
➢ Automatically restoring trust or relationship.
➢ A denial of justice - rather, it entrusts justice to God.

Romans 12:19 reminds us: *"Do not take revenge, my dear friends, but leave room for God's wrath, for it is written: 'It is mine to avenge; I will repay,' says the Lord."*

Forgiveness doesn't mean injustice goes unanswered - it means we stop being judge and executioner and place the matter in God's hands.

The parable of the unforgiving servant

To illustrate this truth, Jesus told a powerful parable in Matthew 18:21-35. Peter had asked, *"Lord, how many times shall I forgive my brother or sister who sins against me? Up to seven times? "Jesus replied, "Not seven times, but seventy-seven times."*

Then He told the story of a servant who owed the king an unpayable debt - ten thousand bags of gold. When he begged for mercy, the king forgave the entire debt. But that same servant went out and found a fellow servant who owed him a small amount - a hundred silver coins - and had him thrown into prison when he couldn't repay. When the king found out, he was furious: *"'You wicked servant,' he said, 'I cancelled all that debt of yours because you begged me to. Shouldn't you have had mercy on your fellow servant just as I had on you?'"* (vv. 32-33). The message here is unmistakable: having been forgiven an infinite debt, we should instinctively extend forgiveness to others.

Forgiveness as a lifestyle

Forgiveness is not a one-time act - it is a lifestyle. People will hurt us, offend us, and disappoint us again and again. And Jesus calls us to keep forgiving. Colossians 3:13 says: "Bear with each other and forgive one another if any of you has a grievance against someone. Forgive as the Lord forgave you."

This means that forgiveness becomes a reflex - a disposition of the heart, and not merely a reaction to extreme circumstances. It means cultivating a posture of grace in all our relationships, big and small.

Forgiveness is one of the most powerful ways we bear witness to the gospel. When we forgive, we show the world what grace looks like. We reflect the heart of our Saviour.

What if I don't feel like forgiving?

Forgiveness is not just a feeling - it is a decision. And often, it is a decision we must make before our emotions catch up. Jesus didn't say, *"When you feel ready, forgive."* He simply and clearly said, *"Forgive."* No more, no less.

This does not mean we deny our pain. It means we choose to surrender it to God. We say, *"Lord, I don't feel like forgiving - but I choose to release this person to You. Help me walk in this decision."* As we continue to pray that prayer, God softens our hearts. He replaces bitterness with peace. He does in us what we cannot do on our own. Forgiveness may be a process - especially in cases of deep trauma or betrayal. But it begins with a decision. And God is faithful to honour and empower that choice.

When we pray, *"Forgive us our sins, as we forgive those who sin against us,"* we are stepping into the flow of God's grace. We are receiving mercy and passing it on. We are joining the rhythm of the kingdom, where forgiveness is both gift and calling. To forgive is not to pretend - it is to proclaim. It is to declare, by faith, that Christ's grace is stronger than the wound, deeper than the pain, and greater than the debt. And as we walk this path, we become more like Jesus - who from the cross cried out, *"Father, forgive them."*

Forgiveness and reconciliation

Forgiveness and reconciliation are deeply related, but not identical. Forgiveness is something we can offer unilaterally - we can forgive someone who never apologizes, who never admits their wrong, or someone who may no longer even be in our lives. Reconciliation, however, will require both parties. It depends on mutual honesty, repentance, and a willingness to rebuild trust.

Romans 12:18 encourages us: *"If it is possible, as far as it depends on you, live at peace with everyone."* Sometimes reconciliation is possible and beautiful as relationships are healed, families are restored, churches are renewed. But sometimes, for reasons that are beyond our control, full reconciliation is not achievable.

Even so, forgiveness must still be given freely, or bitterness will fester. Forgiveness will open the door to reconciliation. It creates the possibility for peace. But even when reconciliation doesn't happen, forgiveness still sets us free.

Forgiveness and freedom

Unforgiveness is a prison. It ties us to the past, chains us to the person who hurt us, and poisons our present with resentment. But true forgiveness breaks those chains. When we forgive, we're not excusing the harm. We are choosing to live in freedom rather than remain enslaved to the offence. We are refusing to let bitterness take root.

Hebrews 12:15 warns: *"See to it that no one falls short of the grace of God and that no bitter root grows up to cause trouble and defile many."* Bitterness doesn't stay contained. It grows, spreads, and infects other areas of our life. But forgiveness cuts it off at the root. It reclaims our hearts for peace, not vengeance. We may think we are protecting ourselves by holding onto the pain. But the truth is, we're healing ourselves by letting it go.

The practice of forgiveness in daily life

Forgiveness isn't just for life's major betrayals - it's also needed in the small, daily interactions that may irritate, wound, or just disappoint us. A careless word. A forgotten promise. A repeated annoyance. In marriage, family life, church community - they all require frequent, deliberate forgiveness.

Colossians 3:13 says: *"Bear with each other and forgive one another if any of you has a grievance against someone. Forgive as the Lord forgave you."* This isn't an occasional act - it's a lifestyle. When we live with this mindset, we become less reactive and more gracious. We don't keep score. We don't hold grudges. We become quick to say, *"I forgive you."* And quicker still to say, *"I'm sorry."*

The Lord's Prayer invites us to build forgiveness into the rhythm of our daily relationship with God - because we need it its power daily, and we need to offer it daily.

When forgiveness feels impossible

Some of us carry wounds so deep that the idea of forgiving feels impossible. The betrayal, the abuse, the injustice - it was real. It hurt. It may still hurt. Forgiveness doesn't mean pretending the pain is gone. It doesn't mean restoring a toxic relationship or ignoring wise boundaries. It means placing the wound in the hands of a God Who sees, Who knows, and Who heals.

Isaiah 61:1 speaks of the mission of Jesus: *"He has sent me to bind up the broken-hearted... to proclaim freedom for the captives and release from darkness for the prisoners."* Only Jesus can do that. And only His Spirit can empower us to forgive what we cannot forgive on our own. If that's where you are, start with this prayer: *"Lord, I'm willing to be made willing."* That's all it takes to begin. He will do the rest.

Forgiveness and the cross

All of this - the forgiveness we receive and the forgiveness we give - finds its centre at the cross. There, Jesus bore our sins. There, He cried, *"Father, forgive them."* There, justice and mercy met. And there, we find the power to live this prayer.

Ephesians 4:32 says: *"Be kind and compassionate to one another, forgiving each other, just as in Christ God forgave you."* That last phrase is key: just as in Christ God forgave you. We forgive, not because others deserve it, but because we didn't either. We forgive, not because the pain wasn't real, but because the grace of Christ is more powerful than our pain. At the foot of the cross, we receive mercy - and we are called to extend it.

Living a forgiven and forgiving Life

When we build this prayer into our lives, we become people who are both honest about our sin and confident in God's grace. We stop pretending. We stop hiding. We live in the freedom of being fully known and fully loved. And when we forgive others, we proclaim the gospel with our lives. We live as signs of the kingdom. We become ministers of reconciliation.

Paul reminds us in 2 Corinthians 5:18, *"All this is from God, who reconciled us to himself through Christ and gave us the ministry of reconciliation."* We are not just forgiven people - we are sent people. People who carry the grace we've received into a world desperate for mercy.

Conclusion

"Forgive us our sins, as we forgive those who sin against us." These words are both invitation and instruction. They draw us into the grace of God and then call us to give that grace away. So let us pray them daily, humbly, and sincerely. Let us confess freely, receive deeply, and forgive boldly - because that is the way of the kingdom. That is the way of Jesus.

9. 'LEAD US NOT INTO TEMPTATION'

A sobering shift in the prayer

As we come to the sixth petition in The Lord's Prayer - *"Lead us not into temptation"* - we encounter a noticeable shift. Earlier petitions have focused on God's name, God's kingdom, God's will, and then our needs for provision and forgiveness. But here, Jesus moves us into a more sobering space - the realm of spiritual danger.

This part of the prayer acknowledges a fundamental truth: life is a battlefield. The Christian life is not a casual walk through a peaceful garden. We are on a journey through enemy territory. Temptation is real, powerful, and persistent - and if we are not vigilant, we can easily be overcome.

So Jesus teaches us to pray proactively. Not, *"Rescue me after I've fallen,"* but *"Lord, don't even let me get near the edge."* For us to fully understand this petition, we need to unpack both what it does and does not mean - and why it's so crucial to the life of every believer.

Does God lead us into temptation?

This petition has confused many readers throughout history because it appears to imply that God might be the one leading us into temptation. But Scripture makes it very clear that this is never the case. James makes this very clear: *"When tempted, no one should say, 'God is tempting me.' For God cannot be tempted by evil, nor does he tempt anyone; but each person is tempted when they are dragged away by their own evil desire and enticed."* (James 1:13-14)

God never tempts us. Temptation is the work of the enemy and the outworking of our fallen nature. So why would Jesus instruct us to pray this way? The phrase *"Lead us not into temptation"* is a Hebrew idiom - a way of expressing a plea for divine protection. It's not suggesting that God would actively tempt us. Rather, it is a humble request that He would guide us away from situations where we are likely to fall. It is a cry for shepherding.

We are saying, *"Lord, don't let me wander into dangerous places. Don't let me be drawn into sin. Steer me toward righteousness and away from harm."*

The nature of temptation

Temptation is the enticement to sin - to turn away from God's will and pursue something that seems pleasurable, convenient, or powerful but leads to destruction. Temptation is not sin in itself - even Jesus was tempted (Matthew 4:1-11), yet He was able to remain sinless. So the danger is not in being tempted, but in yielding to it.

Temptation usually comes in three forms, as described by John: *"For everything in the world - the lust of the flesh, the lust of the eyes, and the pride of life - comes not from the Father, but from the world."* (1 John 2:16). These correspond to the three temptations which Jesus faced in the wilderness:

➢ Lust of the flesh: *"Turn these stones to bread."*
➢ Lust of the eyes: *"All these kingdoms I will give You."*
➢ Pride of life: *"Throw Yourself down - the angels will catch You."*

Temptation always whispers the same lie: *"You can have what you want without trusting God."*

The Danger of self-reliance

Jesus teaches us to pray this line because He knows that we are vulnerable. Left to ourselves, we are not strong enough to resist every temptation. Pride tells us we're fine - that we can handle it. But this petition teaches us to pray from a posture of humility and dependence.

1 Corinthians 10:12–13 gives both warning and hope: *"So, if you think you are standing firm, be careful that you don't fall! No temptation has overtaken you except what is common to mankind. And God is faithful; he will not let you be tempted beyond what you can bear. But when you are tempted, he will also provide a way out so that you can endure it."*

The danger is real - but so is the provision. God offers us strength to resist and a way of escape. But we must seek it. And that's what this petition is about - training our hearts to ask for help before the storm comes.

Jesus, our High Priest Who understands

One of the most comforting truths for believers is that Jesus Himself understands temptation. He endured it in its full force - not just the surface-level allure but the deep spiritual attack that accompanies it. Hebrews 4:15 says: "*For we do not have a high priest who is unable to empathize with our weaknesses, but we have one who has been tempted in every way, just as we are - yet he did not sin.*"

This means we never face temptation alone. When we cry out, "*Lead us not into temptation,*" we cry to a Saviour who knows the battle. He has walked the path. He has faced the enemy. And He has triumphed.

That's why the very next verse in Hebrews says: "*Let us then approach God's throne of grace with confidence, so that we may receive mercy and find grace to help us in our time of need.*" (Hebrews 4:16). We are not left to fend for ourselves. We are invited to lean on Jesus - to seek His wisdom, His power, His Spirit. That's exactly what this line of the prayer invites us to do.

Temptation and the testing of faith

It's also important to recognize that in Scripture, the same Greek word *(peirasmos)* can mean both temptation and testing. The difference lies not in the experience, but in the intent.

➤ Temptation seeks to destroy.
➤ Testing seeks to refine.

God does not tempt, but He does allow tests. Not to make us fall, but to strengthen our faith. As James reminds us: "*Consider it pure joy, my brothers and sisters, whenever you face trials of many kinds, because you know that the testing of your faith produces perseverance. Let perseverance finish its work so that you may be mature and complete, not lacking anything.*" (James 1:2-4).

So when we pray, *"Lead us not into temptation,"* we are not asking God to spare us from all hardship. We are asking Him to spare us from the kind of testing that would exceed our strength. We are asking Him to keep us near, to guide us through trials without letting them become traps.

"Lead us not into temptation." This is not the prayer of the proud, but of the wise. It is the prayer of the humble who know the danger of sin and the deceitfulness of the enemy. It is a cry for protection, for vigilance, for God's guiding hand. Jesus does not teach us to live in fear, but He does teach us to live in awareness. Temptation is real. The enemy is real. Our weakness is real. But so is God's power, God's Spirit, and God's promises.

So we pray: *"Father, lead me. Lead me away from the cliff's edge. Lead me into paths of righteousness. Guard my heart. Strengthen my spirit. Keep me close. Lead me not into temptation."*

God's provision for resisting temptation

When we ask God not to lead us into temptation, we are not passively waiting for Him to remove all dangers from our path. We are praying for the wisdom and strength to resist when temptation does come - and we do so confident in God's promise to help us.

As we saw in 1 Corinthians 10:13: *"God is faithful; he will not let you be tempted beyond what you can bear. But when you are tempted, he will also provide a way out so that you can endure it."* This verse is a precious promise. Every temptation comes with an exit sign - a God-given way to flee. Our responsibility is to look for that way and to take it. But in our own strength, we may not even see it.

That's why we pray. We need the Spirit to awaken our spiritual senses, alert us to danger, and point us toward the path of escape. When we pray "Lead us not into temptation," we are actually saying: *"Lord, don't let me be blind to danger. Don't let me justify compromise. Don't let me rationalize sin. Help me to flee and stand."*

Watch and pray: The words of Jesus in Gethsemane

On the night He was betrayed, Jesus gave a direct command to His disciples that echoes this petition. In Matthew 26:41, He said: *"Watch and pray so that you will not fall into temptation. The spirit is willing, but the flesh is weak."* Here we see the two really important components of us resisting temptation: vigilance and prayer.

> ➢ *Watch* - Be alert. Know your weaknesses. Discern the enemy's schemes.
> ➢ *Pray* - Draw near to God, your source of strength. Ask for help before the trial strikes.

Jesus knew that His disciples were about to face their greatest test - and He wanted them prepared. But instead of watching and praying, they slept. And when the hour of trial came, they scattered. We are no different. Unless we are spiritually awake and prayerful, we will be caught off guard. But the good news is that prayer keeps us anchored. This petition in The Lord's Prayer is our daily reminder to be ready and reliant.

Know your weaknesses

Each of us is uniquely vulnerable to certain kinds of temptation. What one believer easily resists may be a significant struggle for another. The enemy is strategic. He studies us. He attacks where we are weakest - not strongest. That's why we must be honest about our vulnerabilities and ask for help in those specific areas. Proverbs 4:23 says: *"Above all else, guard your heart, for everything you do flows from it."* Knowing our hearts helps us recognize where temptation is most likely to strike:

> ➢ For some, it's lust or sexual impurity.
> ➢ For others, it's greed or materialism
> ➢ Others wrestle with anger, pride, envy, gossip, or self-pity.

When we pray *"Lead us not into temptation,"* we are saying: *"God, You know where I'm weak. You know what triggers me. Guard me. Guide me. Keep me far from the traps the enemy lays in those areas."*

This prayer is not general. It's highly specific. It invites us to identify our battle zones and surrender them to the Spirit of God.

The role of the Word of God

One of the most powerful weapons in resisting temptation is always the Word of God. Jesus Himself demonstrated this during His wilderness temptation in Matthew 4. When Satan tempted Him, He responded three times with: *"It is written..."* He didn't argue. He didn't explain. He stood on the Word.

Psalm 119:11 says: *"I have hidden your word in my heart that I might not sin against you."* The more Scripture we internalize, the more resilient we become. When lies come, we can counter them with truth. When temptation whispers, *"No one will know,"* God's Word reminds us, *"Nothing in all creation is hidden from God's sight."* (Hebrews 4:13). When sin promises happiness, the Bible declares that *"sin gives birth to death"* (James 1:15). This is why a regular intake of the Scriptures - through reading, memorization, meditation - is essential. It fortifies our minds and renews our desires. God's Word doesn't just inform us; it transforms us.

The power of community

One of the great lies of temptation is that we're all alone. The enemy thrives in secrecy and isolation. But God designed us for community - to walk together, fight together, and support one another. Ecclesiastes 4:9-10 says: *"Two are better than one... If either of them falls down, one can help the other up. But pity anyone who falls and has no one to help them up."*

James 5:16 encourages: *"Therefore confess your sins to each other and pray for each other so that you may be healed."* When we hide, temptation gains strength. But when we bring our struggles into the light, they begin to lose their power. There is healing in confession, accountability, and intercessory prayer. This petition - *"Lead us not into temptation"* - is not just a private prayer. It's a corporate prayer. Jesus teaches us to pray, *"Lead us not into temptation."* We are meant to pray for one another, support one another, and walk together in the pursuit of holiness.

Guarding the gateways

Temptation often enters our lives through the gateways of the senses - what we see, hear, read, and consume. Therefore, part of resisting temptation involves guarding those gates. Jesus said: *"The eye is the lamp of the body. If your eyes are healthy, your whole body will be full of light. But if your eyes are unhealthy, your whole body will be full of darkness."* (Matthew 6:22-23)

What we watch, listen to, scroll through, and engage with shapes our thoughts and desires. If we feed ourselves constantly with worldly messages, provocative images, or divisive voices, we make ourselves more vulnerable to temptation. So praying *"Lead us not into temptation"* must be matched with wise choices about what we allow into our minds and hearts. Ask questions like:

➢ Am I setting myself up for temptation by my media habits?

➢ Am I placing myself in environments where sin is easy?

➢ Do I need to make practical changes to safeguard my purity, peace, or integrity?

The Holy Spirit often leads us through simple acts of wisdom - changing our routines, setting boundaries, removing triggers. Temptation thrives on unguarded moments. So we must always be watchful.

So when we pray, *"Lead us not into temptation,"* we are not only asking God to steer us away from spiritual danger – we are committing ourselves to live a life of vigilance, dependence, discipline, and wisdom. God gives us the means:

➢ His Spirit to empower us

➢ His Word to ground us

➢ His people to walk with us

➢ His grace to sustain us

Temptation is part of the journey. But it does not have to define us. By God's strength, we can stand firm. And by His mercy, we can rise when we fall.

When temptation comes anyway

Though we pray to be spared from temptation, we know that it often still comes. Trials and enticements are an unavoidable part of life in a fallen world. Even Jesus, in His perfect obedience, was led by the Spirit into the wilderness - where He was tempted by the devil (Matthew 4:1). But unlike us, Jesus did not sin. So what do we do when temptation does arrive?

We remember that God is still present. He is not caught off guard. He is not distant. He has already made provision for that moment through His Word, His Spirit, and His people. The presence of temptation is not evidence that God has abandoned us. In fact, sometimes it is precisely in the moment of testing that we come to rely most deeply on His strength. Psalm 46:1 reminds us: *"God is our refuge and strength, an ever-present help in trouble."* Even in the fire of temptation, He is near - and He is strong.

The example and victory of Christ

In Matthew 4, when Jesus was tempted by Satan, He overcame not by calling down angels or displaying divine power, but by standing on the Word of God. Each time the devil twisted truth, Jesus answered with Scripture. This shows us that Jesus not only knows our struggle - He has triumphed over it.

Hebrews 2:18 tells us: *"Because he himself suffered when he was tempted, he is able to help those who are being tempted."* Christ's victory over temptation is not just a model - it is a means. Because He overcame, we are now in Him, and His power becomes our power. Romans 6:14 says: *"For sin shall no longer be your master, because you are not under the law, but under grace."* We are not slaves to sin. In Christ, we have the power to resist. We are no longer doomed to failure - we are equipped for victory.

When we fall

But what happens when we don't resist? What happens when temptation overcomes us and we sin? Jesus taught us to pray not only, *"Lead us not into temptation,"* but also, *"Forgive us our sins."* He knew that in our weakness, we would sometimes fall.

And He provided a path back. 1 John 1:9 is the promise we cling to in those moments: *"If we confess our sins, he is faithful and just and will forgive us our sins and purify us from all unrighteousness."* There is grace for the fallen. Always.

Peter knew this from personal experience. He vowed never to deny Jesus yet did exactly that three times in the one night. But Jesus restored him, commissioned him, and used him mightily. Why? Because failure is never final in the kingdom of God. When we fall, we don't run from God - we run to Him. We confess. We repent. We receive mercy. And we begin again.

God's commitment to our sanctification

As we continue to pray this prayer - *"Lead us not into temptation"* - we are participating in a process called sanctification. This is God's work of making us holy - conforming us to the image of Christ. Philippians 1:6 gives us this confidence: *"Being confident of this, that he who began a good work in you will carry it on to completion until the day of Christ Jesus."*

God is committed to your growth. He doesn't just forgive you once and leave you unchanged. He shapes your desires. He matures your responses. He deepens your reliance on Him. Over time, you may still face the same temptations but your response changes. Your roots go deeper. Your reflexes grow stronger. Your dependence on grace becomes more consistent. This daily prayer is not only protection - it is formation. It shapes us into people who are aware of spiritual danger, honest about our limitations, and deeply anchored in divine strength.

Deliverance in the final temptation

While this part of the prayer focuses on daily battles, it also hints at something bigger: the ultimate temptation - the final testing that may come near the end of life, or in the last days of this age. Some scholars believe this line of the prayer is eschatological - a plea for God to spare us from the great testing that will mark the end of the age. In Matthew 24:21, Jesus speaks of a time of *"great distress"* that will come upon the earth.

Whether or not we live to see that time, the prayer reminds us to ask not only for daily preservation but for final perseverance. That we would be kept faithful all the way to the end.

Jesus said in Matthew 24:13, *"But the one who stands firm to the end will be saved."* This petition is a prayer for endurance. Not just to resist temptation today, but to stay faithful for life.

The hope of final victory

One day, the battle with temptation will be over. Revelation 21:27 says: *"Nothing impure will ever enter [the New Jerusalem], nor will anyone who does what is shameful or deceitful, but only those whose names are written in the Lamb's book of life."*

No more sin. No more struggle. No more traps, lies, no more seductions. The enemy will finally be silenced. The flesh will be transformed. The world will be made new. Until then, we pray: *"Father, lead me. Guide me. Protect me. Help me to stand."*

Practical Encouragement for the Journey

In closing this chapter, here are a few final encouragements:

> *Keep praying it:* Make this line a regular part of your devotional life. Say it with sincerity and watch how God shapes your path.

> *Don't be surprised by temptation:* It is not a sign of spiritual failure to be tempted. It is a sign that you are human - and in the fight.

> *Use your tools:* The Word of God, the Spirit of God, the people of God - these are your daily companions in the battle.

> *When you fall, rise quickly:* The enemy wants you stuck in guilt. But grace lifts you up.

> *Fix your eyes on Jesus:* He is your example, your helper, and your victory.

Conclusion

"Lead us not into temptation." It's not just a defensive request. It's a declaration of trust. A confession of need. A desire to walk close to the Shepherd who guides us through the valley of shadows and leads us in paths of righteousness.

In a world filled with enticements and snares, this prayer trains our hearts to seek God's way over the world's. To rely on grace over grit. To remember that our help does not come from ourselves - but from the Lord, who is able to keep us from falling and to present us blameless before His glorious presence with great joy. Let us pray it daily. Let us live it honestly. Let us walk humbly - and victoriously - in the strength of our God.

10. 'DELIVER US FROM THE EVIL ONE'

A prayer for protection in a dangerous world

As we come to the final petition in the Lord's Prayer, Jesus brings us face-to-face with one of the most sobering realities of our faith: evil is not an abstract idea - it is a present, personal threat. This is not merely a prayer for protection from generic harm. It is a desperate, urgent appeal to God to rescue us from the one who is actively working to destroy our souls: *"the evil one."*

Jesus taught us to pray this way because He knew the reality of spiritual warfare. He knew that our lives are not lived on neutral ground. We are in a contested space, surrounded by unseen enemies, and we need divine intervention every single day. We need rescue. This part of the prayer reminds us that the Christian life is not only about inward growth or outward service - it is also about battle. To ignore this truth is to become easy prey. But to embrace it with faith and vigilance is to walk in the victory of Christ.

The evil one: real, personal, and active

Jesus didn't say, *"Deliver us from evil"* in a general sense (though some translations render it that way). The Greek phrase is *"tou ponērou"* - a masculine form that points not to an abstract force, but to a specific person. It is rightly translated: *"the evil one."*

The New Testament consistently presents Satan as a very real, personal being - a fallen angel, a liar, a murderer, the accuser of the brethren, and the adversary of God's people. Jesus referred to him plainly:

"You belong to your father, the devil, and you want to carry out your father's desires. He was a murderer from the beginning, not holding to the truth, for there is no truth in him. When he lies, he speaks his native language, for he is a liar and the father of lies."(John 8:44). Satan is not some cartoon figure in red tights holding a pitchfork. He is a cunning, spiritual being who hates God and seeks to ruin every image-bearer of God - that includes you and me.

The work of the Evil One

So what does the evil one do? The Bible provides us with a pretty clear job description:

- ➤ He deceives: (Genesis 3:1-5; 2 Corinthians 11:3)
- ➤ He twists truth to plant doubt in our minds about God's goodness and Word.
- ➤ He accuses: (Revelation 12:10)
- ➤ He reminds us of our sins and failures to drown us in guilt and shame.
- ➤ He tempts: (Matthew 4:1-11)
- ➤ He lures us away from obedience with promises of pleasure, power, or safety.
- ➤ He blinds: (2 Corinthians 4:4)
- ➤ He darkens the minds of unbelievers so they cannot see the light of the gospel.
- ➤ He devours: (1 Peter 5:8)
- ➤ He is likened to a roaring lion, seeking to destroy lives, faith, and witness.

When we pray, *"deliver us from the evil one,"* we are confessing and acknowledging that left to ourselves, we are no match for such a formidable enemy. We need divine protection, not just from sin but from the one who orchestrates sin.

Deliverance: Not just protection, but rescue

The word *"deliver"* in this petition is from the Greek *"rhuomai,"* which means to rescue, to snatch away, to draw out from danger. This is not just a prayer for our general safety. It's a plea for God to intervene decisively - to pull us out of harm's way, even when we're unaware of how close we are to destruction.

Think of Lot being dragged out of Sodom before judgment fell (Genesis 19:16), or Peter being delivered from prison by an angel (Acts 12:7). That's the kind of dramatic, merciful, and powerful rescue Jesus teaches us to seek.

We are not asking for a calm spiritual life - we are asking to be rescued from disaster. This is not polite language. It is the cry of a soul who knows the enemy is near.

Jesus, our deliverer

This petition is answered not just in principle but in a Person. Jesus Christ is our deliverer. Paul says, *"For he has rescued us from the dominion of darkness and brought us into the kingdom of the Son he loves, in whom we have redemption, the forgiveness of sins."* (Colossians 1:13-14). The cross was the ultimate and powerful act of deliverance. There, Jesus disarmed the powers of darkness, broke the grip of the enemy, and freed us from the penalty and power of sin.

Hebrews 2:14-15 echoes this: *"Since the children have flesh and blood, he too shared in their humanity so that by his death he might break the power of him who holds the power of death - that is, the devil - and free those who all their lives were held in slavery by their fear of death."* When we pray this line from The Lord's Prayer, we are appealing to the One who has already triumphed. We are not begging for something uncertain - we are claiming what Christ has already won.

The ongoing battle: Already won, but not yet over

Though Jesus defeated Satan decisively at the cross, the enemy still roams – just like a defeated general who refuses to accept surrender. He is still active in the world today, still fighting, still deceiving. But he is on a leash. His time is short, and his defeat is sure. Revelation 12:12 warns: *"He is filled with fury, because he knows that his time is short."*

That's why the battle sometimes intensifies - because the enemy is desperate. But it's also why our confidence should grow - because the victory is certain. So we pray daily: *"Deliver us from the evil one."* Not in fear, but in faith. Not in panic, but in trust. Not because we're unsure - but because we want to walk in the victory that is already ours in Christ.

Spiritual warfare and the armour of God

Paul gives us a clear view of this battle: *"Finally, be strong in the Lord and in his mighty power. Put on the full armour of God, so that you can take your stand against the devil's schemes. For our struggle is not against flesh and blood, but against the rulers, against the authorities, against the powers of this dark world and against the spiritual forces of evil in the heavenly realms."* (Ephesians 6:10–13)

We are never called to fight in our own strength. We are called to stand in the strength of the Lord. This is why prayer is so important - it connects us to the actual power of God. And the armour Paul lists - truth, righteousness, the gospel of peace, faith, salvation, the Word, and prayer – are not defensive accessories. They are divinely empowered tools for victory. To pray *"deliver us from the evil one"* is to ask God to clothe us daily in His armour, and to teach us how to stand firm when the enemy attacks.

The final petition of The Lord's Prayer opens our eyes to a spiritual reality we cannot afford to ignore. There is an enemy - a personal, cunning, relentless enemy - and he seeks to destroy us. But we are not left defenceless. We have a Deliverer. We have a Saviour. We have a Protector. We have a King who has already won the battle.

When we pray, *"Deliver us from the evil one,"* we are not praying as victims - we are praying as soldiers under the command of the victorious Christ. We pray with open eyes, humbled hearts, and confident faith.

The battle is real - but so is the escape

Temptation, deception, and spiritual warfare are not just theoretical ideas for theologians or pastors - they are the daily experience of every believer. But Jesus didn't teach us to pray out of fear. He taught us to pray with confidence in God's protection and power. Paul reminds us in 2 Thessalonians 3:3: *"But the Lord is faithful, and he will strengthen you and protect you from the evil one."* That promise is deeply reassuring. God does not leave us to fend for ourselves.

He does not abandon us in the spiritual trenches. Every time we pray, *"deliver us from the evil one,"* we are calling on our faithful Deliverer who is both willing and able to protect His children. But how does that deliverance actually happen? What does it look like when God answers this prayer?

Deliverance through discernment

One way God delivers us is by giving us spiritual discernment - the ability to recognize the enemy's schemes before they take hold. Satan is a master of disguise. Paul says in 2 Corinthians 11:14: *"Satan himself masquerades as an angel of light."* That's what makes his work so dangerous. He doesn't always come with horns and fire – all too often, he comes with charm, subtlety, and plausibility. God's enemy convinces us that wrong is right, that compromise is wise, that sin is harmless.

But the Holy Spirit sharpens our perception. He helps us detect the false note in what sounds appealing. He alerts us to spiritual danger. This is one reason why prayer is so important - it keeps our minds tuned to directly to God's voice. Hebrews 5:14 praises the spiritually mature: *"But solid food is for the mature, who by constant use have trained themselves to distinguish good from evil."* Discernment is a form of deliverance. It will keep us from being fooled. It will open our eyes so we can avoid the enemy's traps before they spring.

Deliverance through resistance

Another way God delivers us is by giving us strength to resist. James 4:7 declares: *"Submit yourselves, then, to God. Resist the devil, and he will flee from you."* That is a stunning promise. Satan is powerful, yes - but he is not invincible. When we stand firm in submission to God, the devil is then forced to flee. He cannot withstand the authority of Christ in us. But notice the important order: *"Submit… then resist."*

We cannot resist the evil one if we are resisting God. Deliverance begins with surrender. Only a life aligned with God's will, can stand strong against Satan's pressure.

Ephesians 6:13 confirms this: *"Therefore put on the full armour of God, so that when the day of evil comes, you may be able to stand your ground, and after you have done everything, to stand."* To stand our ground is to not give in - not to fear, not to sin, not to retreat. By God's grace, we resist.

Deliverance through the Word

When Jesus was tempted by the devil in the wilderness, He did not rely on clever arguments or brute spiritual force. Instead, He responded each time with a simple, powerful phrase: *"It is written."* Three times in Matthew 4, Jesus resisted Satan by quoting Scripture. This shows us that God delivers His people through His Word.

Psalm 119:105 reminds us: *"Your word is a lamp for my feet, a light on my path."* When we're surrounded by darkness, deception, and confusion, Scripture brings clarity. When the enemy tempts us to despair, the Word speaks hope. When he accuses, the Word reminds us that we are forgiven. When he lies, the Word tells the truth.

But for the Word to help us in the heat of battle, it must be hidden in our hearts. We must read it, meditate on it, memorize it. That's how the sword of the Spirit is kept sharp and ready. Paul says: *"Take the helmet of salvation and the sword of the Spirit, which is the word of God."* (Ephesians 6:17). In God's hands, the Word is always not just a source of wisdom - but a weapon of war.

Deliverance through prayer

It should not surprise us that the final line of The Lord's Prayer is itself a prayer for deliverance. Prayer is not only a response to the attack - it is our first line of defence. Jesus told His disciples in the garden, *"Watch and pray so that you will not fall into temptation."* (Matthew 26:41). He was saying: *"You cannot survive this night without prayer."* And they didn't. Satan is not afraid of our good intentions. He's not intimidated by our spiritual knowledge or past experiences. But he trembles when we pray. Why? Because prayer places us under God's protection.

Prayer invites the presence of the Spirit. Prayer brings the power of heaven into the battles of earth. The more we pray, the less vulnerable we are. The less we pray, the more we risk defeat.

Deliverance through the fellowship of believers

God also delivers us through the people He places in our lives. Ecclesiastes 4:12 says: *"Though one may be overpowered, two can defend themselves. A cord of three strands is not quickly broken."* We are not meant to fight the enemy alone. The church is not a collection of isolated warriors - it is really an army. We protect each other. We watch each other's blind spots. We pray for one another. We offer truth when one is tempted and grace when one has fallen.

James 5:16 encourages us: *"Therefore confess your sins to each other and pray for each other so that you may be healed."* Deliverance sometimes comes through accountability. Sometimes it comes through a word of warning, encouragement, or timely correction from a brother or sister in Christ. To walk in victory over the evil one, we really need community. We need people who help us remember who we are and whose we are.

Deliverance through the blood of the Lamb

Ultimately, our confidence in deliverance comes not from our own strength, but from the finished work of Christ. Satan's power over us was broken at the cross. Revelation 12:11 declares: *"They triumphed over him by the blood of the Lamb and by the word of their testimony; they did not love their lives so much as to shrink from death."* The blood of Jesus is our protection. It is our covering, our cleansing, and our confidence. When the evil one accuses, we point to the cross. When he threatens, we declare that we are not our own - we have been bought with a price. There is no stronger shield, no greater power, no deeper freedom than what Christ accomplished at Calvary.

When we pray, *"Deliver us from the evil one,"* we are calling on the name of the God who sees every ambush, knows every trap, and holds the power to rescue us from them all.

His deliverance may come through discernment, resistance, Scripture, prayer, community, or a miracle. But in whatever form this deliverance comes, it is always rooted in the unshakable victory of Jesus Christ.

Living daily as the delivered

When we pray, *"Deliver us from the evil one,"* we are not only asking for divine rescue in the moment - we are also committing to live each day in the light of that deliverance. Deliverance is not a one-time experience. It's a clear lifestyle. It's a pattern of daily dependence, vigilance, and faith.

As followers of Christ, we must learn to walk as those who have been rescued - not as slaves in hiding, but as children of the light. Paul writes in Ephesians 5:8: *"For you were once darkness, but now you are light in the Lord. Live as children of light."*

This is the call of the delivered: to live as those no longer under Satan's dominion. To refuse to return to the chains that once held us. To shine with holiness in a world darkened by deception. Living daily as the delivered means waking up each morning and saying, *"Lord, I know the enemy is near - but You are nearer. Deliver me today. Keep me close."*

Victory is a process

Some believers get discouraged when they still struggle with temptation, even after praying for deliverance. But it's important to remember that spiritual victory is often a process, not an instant event. God sometimes delivers us immediately - but more often, He delivers us gradually as we walk with Him daily, learning to resist, learning to rely, learning to rest in His power.

The Israelites didn't enter the Promised Land in one day. They had to fight for every inch, relying on God's presence and promises. The same is true for us. We are on a journey of sanctification - where each battle shapes us, strengthens us, and deepens our dependence on Christ.

Philippians 2:12-13 gives us both sides of this truth: *"Continue to work out your salvation with fear and trembling, for it is God who works in you to will and to act in order to fulfill his good purpose."* God is working in us, even when we feel weak. Even when we stumble. He is delivering us, even when the progress seems slow. Our role is to keep showing up, keep praying, and keep trusting.

When the attack comes

There will be days in our journey when the enemy's assault feels overwhelming. You might face sudden temptation, oppressive discouragement, or unexpected spiritual confusion. It's in those moments that the prayer, *"Deliver us from the evil one"* becomes most urgent - and most powerful. What should we do in those moments?

➢ *Speak Scripture aloud:* Declare the truth of God's Word. The spoken Word wields spiritual power. (Ephesians 6:17)

➢ *Call on the name of Jesus:* There is power in His name - to calm storms, to silence demons, and to drive out fear. (Philippians 2:9-11)

➢ *Reach out to a fellow believer:* Don't suffer alone. One word of prayer or encouragement can turn the tide. (Ecclesiastes 4:10)

➢ *Stand still and remember the cross:* Satan's power was broken there. He cannot condemn you. He cannot possess you. You belong to Christ. (Romans 8:1)

You are not without weapons. You are not without defence. The Lord hears the cries of His people, and He knows how to deliver. 2 Peter 2:9 affirms: *"The Lord knows how to rescue the godly from trials..."* We don't have to figure out the escape route. He already knows it. He already holds it.

Deliverance leads to witness

One often-overlooked outcome of God's deliverance is our witness to others. When you walk through spiritual attack - and come out on the other side - you become a testimony of God's faithfulness.

You become a living picture of His power and grace. You can say with Paul in 2 Timothy 4:18: *"The Lord will rescue me from every evil attack and will bring me safely to his heavenly kingdom. To him be glory for ever and ever. Amen."*

Your deliverance is not just for you. It becomes fuel for someone else's faith. It becomes a reminder to the church that we are not forsaken, not abandoned, and never powerless. One of the most powerful ways to declare God's goodness is simply to say, *"I was under attack - but He delivered me."*

Deliverance and humility

There is no room for spiritual arrogance when you pray, *"Deliver us from the evil one."* That prayer begins in humility - it is really a confession that we simply cannot deliver ourselves. We are not invincible. We are not ever strong enough, wise enough, or good enough to resist the enemy without divine help.

This prayer keeps us grounded. It reminds us that we are always in need of grace. It puts us in the posture of a child calling out to their Father - not in fear, but in trust.

James 4:6–7 says: *"God opposes the proud but shows favour to the humble. Submit yourselves, then, to God. Resist the devil, and he will flee from you."* Only the humble are delivered. Only the submitted can resist. So we kneel before the Father and say: *"Lord, I'm vulnerable. Lead me, guard me, deliver me. You are my only hope."*

The final deliverance

While we pray for daily deliverance, there is also a final deliverance coming - when God will once and for all rid His creation of evil, and Satan will be cast down forever. Revelation 20:10 declares: *"And the devil, who deceived them, was thrown into the lake of burning sulphur... They will be tormented day and night for ever and ever."* The day is coming when the evil one will no longer prowl. His voice will no longer accuse you. His power will be extinguished. And God's people will be safe forever. Until then, we pray. We resist. We persevere.

As Paul wrote in Romans 16:20: *"The God of peace will soon crush Satan under your feet. The grace of our Lord Jesus be with you."*

Ending Where Jesus Began

As we reflect on this final petition, we find that it ties back to the very beginning of The Lord's Prayer. We began with: *"Our Father in heaven, hallowed be your name."* And now we end with: *"Deliver us from the evil one."* The Lord's Prayer moves from adoration to dependence, from reverence to our rescue. It begins with God's greatness and ends with our need - and all the way, it keeps our eyes on Him.

➢ We pray to a Father who is loving.
➢ We trust a kingdom that is unshakeable.
➢ We seek a will that is perfect.
➢ We rely on daily provision, receive daily pardon, and ask for daily protection.

This is not just a prayer - it's a way of life.

Conclusion

The phrase *"Deliver us from the evil one"* is not just a last-minute addition to the prayer. It is a reminder of our vulnerability and a call to trust in divine strength. Jesus placed it here because He knew what His followers would face. He knew how fierce the enemy could be. And He knew how faithful the Father would be to deliver them.

So we pray it with boldness. We live it with awareness. We trust it with confidence. The evil one may rage, but he is already defeated. And every time we pray this prayer, we stand in the shadow of the cross and proclaim: *"Greater is He who is in me than he who is in the world."* (1 John 4:4)

11. 'FOR YOURS IS THE KINGDOM'

The glorious conclusion

Although the words *"For yours is the kingdom and the power and the glory forever. Amen,"* are not in the earliest Greek manuscripts of Matthew's Gospel, they have been embraced by the church for centuries as a fitting and triumphant doxology. Most scholars agree that this concluding phrase reflects biblical truth and is deeply consistent with the themes of the prayer. It beautifully affirms what has been prayed - that all of life, including our needs, our sins, and our struggles, all rest under the sovereign rule of God.

We now turn to the first part of this concluding phrase: *"For yours is the kingdom."* With these words, we are not making a request - we are making a declaration. We are affirming that this entire prayer rests on the foundation of God's kingship. We are saying: *"Lord, we have asked for your name to be hallowed, your will to be done, your provision to be granted, your pardon to be given, and your protection to be extended - because you are the King. Yours is the kingdom."*

A declaration of sovereignty

To say *"Yours is the kingdom"* is to declare that God reigns. He is the King above all kings, the Lord above all lords. His rule is not symbolic or partial - it is absolute. He reigns over all creation: over time and space, over history and humanity, over kings and kingdoms, over angels and demons. Psalm 103:19 states clearly: *"The Lord has established his throne in heaven, and his kingdom rules over all."*

This is not merely poetic. It is theological. God's rule is not theoretical; it is real, active, and unshakable. He governs the world - not as a detached observer, but as a sovereign ruler who is working out His purposes even when we cannot see them. This phrase in The Lord's Prayer is an anchor for our souls. It reminds us that no matter what chaos surrounds us, God still reigns.

A personal acknowledgment of authority

Praying *"Yours is the kingdom"* is not just a statement about God's rule over the universe - it's also a personal confession. It means we are recognizing His authority over our own lives. It's easy to affirm God's rule in theory. But this phrase calls us to lay down our crowns. It invites us to acknowledge that we are not the kings or queens of our own little empires.

We are not the centre of the universe. We are subjects in God's Kingdom. Jesus asks a probing question in Luke 6:46: *"Why do you call me, 'Lord, Lord,' and do not do what I say?"* To confess *"Yours is the kingdom"* is to say, *"Lord, you are the rightful ruler of my heart, my time, my resources, my decisions, my dreams."* It's a surrender. A submission. A relinquishing of control. It is saying: *"This life is not mine. It belongs to you. You are the King - not me."*

The nature of God's kingdom

We dealt with this in Chapter 4 in this book, but let's dig a little deeper. During His earthly ministry, Jesus spoke often of the kingdom of God. In fact, it was the central theme of all His preaching.

Mark 1:15 records His earliest proclamation: *"The time has come,"* he said. *"The kingdom of God has come near. Repent and believe the good news!"* But what kind of kingdom is this?

Unlike earthly kingdoms built on military power, political alliances, or wealth, the kingdom of God is built on truth, righteousness, peace, and love. It's a kingdom that enters quietly, grows steadily, and transforms completely. Jesus described it with a number of different parables:

➢ Like a mustard seed, it starts small but grows large (Matthew 13:31–32).
➢ Like yeast, it works invisibly but changes everything (Matthew 13:33).
➢ Like hidden treasure, it is worth giving up everything to obtain (Matthew 13:44).

The Kingdom of God is not defined by borders, currencies or flags. It is wherever God reigns. And as believers, we are both citizens and ambassadors of this kingdom.

The kingdom is present and future

As I have stressed a number of times, one of the great tensions in Scripture is the *"now but not yet"* nature of the Kingdom. On the one hand, the Kingdom is already here. Jesus said it had come near. It is present wherever Christ is worshipped and His will is done. Every act of mercy, every heart transformed, every life surrendered to Christ is a sign of His reigning presence.

But on the other hand, the Kingdom is not yet fully here. There is still sin, injustice, rebellion, and sorrow. We still wait for the day when Christ will return to consummate His Kingdom - when every knee will bow, and every tongue confess that Jesus is Lord (Philippians 2:10–11).

Revelation 11:15 looks forward to that day: *"The kingdom of the world has become the kingdom of our Lord and of his Messiah, and he will reign for ever and ever."* To say *"Yours is the kingdom"* is to live in hopeful anticipation. We live in a broken world, but we serve a reigning King. His rule is both now and not yet. His throne is occupied, even if not everyone acknowledges it yet.

The Kingdom reframes our prayers

This phrase also reorients how we pray. By ending The Lord's Prayer with *"Yours is the kingdom,"* we are reminded that prayer is not about getting God to serve our kingdom - it's all about aligning our hearts with His. Too often, we approach prayer like consumers - asking for what benefits us the most.

But this declaration pulls us back into the truth: *"This is your kingdom, Lord. Not mine. Let my requests serve your purposes."* It places all petitions - for daily bread, forgiveness, and protection - under the banner of God's Kingdom agenda. It checks our motives and sanctifies our desires.

Are we asking for provision to fuel selfish ambition - or to serve the Kingdom? Are we seeking forgiveness as an excuse for us to continue in sin - or to be restored as servants? Are we pleading for deliverance from times of trouble - or for power to stand firm as Kingdom witnesses? When we say *"Yours is the kingdom,"* we declare that our prayers, like our lives, must revolve around the King and His purposes.

This first phrase of the doxology, *"For yours is the kingdom,"* lifts our eyes to the throne of God and reminds us of who we are and whose we are. It calls us to confess, to surrender, and to rejoice in the eternal reign of the One who is both sovereign over the universe and intimately present in our lives. It is not a timid whisper it is a bold declaration: *"The kingdom belongs to You, Lord - not to me, not to evil, not to chaos, not to rulers or nations or powers - but to You alone."*

Power that is divine, not human

When we proclaim, *"For yours is the power,"* we are making a statement that distinguishes the nature of God's strength from every other form of power we experience. Earthly power is often unstable, corrupt, or limited. It can be abused or lost. Human power rises and falls, but God's power is eternal, pure, and absolute. Psalm 62:11 says: *"One thing God has spoken, two things I have heard: 'Power belongs to you, God.'"*

The Hebrew word here for *"power"* speaks of might, strength, and force - but unlike human might, God's power is always righteous, always just, always aligned with His goodness. We live in a culture obsessed with strength: political power, social influence, economic dominance, and even personal control. But Jesus reminds us that all true power belongs to God. Not to Caesar. Not to emperors, presidents, or systems. Not even to the devil.

Power ultimately flows from and returns to the throne of heaven. To say *"Yours is the power"* is to lay aside our illusion of control and to confess that all we have, all we are, and all we need - comes from the hand of an all-powerful God.

Power displayed in creation

God's power is first revealed in creation. The opening pages of Scripture declare a God who speaks, and worlds appear. No materials. No helpers. No effort. Just a word. Genesis 1:3: *"And God said, 'Let there be light,' and there was light."* Psalm 33:6 affirms: *"By the word of the Lord the heavens were made, their starry host by the breath of his mouth."*

There is no act more powerful than the act of creating something out of nothing. When we pray *"Yours is the power,"* we are really acknowledging that the One we are speaking to is the same One Who set galaxies spinning, formed mountains, sculpted oceans, and breathed life into humanity.

This is not a frail, far-off deity. This is the Lord of all creation. His power is visible in every sunrise, every thunderstorm, every heartbeat, and every breath.

Power revealed in redemption

While creation displays God's raw power, redemption reveals His restoring power. The greatest demonstration of divine power is not in the forming of stars - but in the saving of sinners. *"For I am not ashamed of the gospel, because it is the power of God that brings salvation to everyone who believes..."* (Romans 1:16). The cross of Christ is not weakness - it is strength in its most astonishing form. When Jesus died, it looked like defeat. But it was the ultimate victory over sin, death, and the evil one.

1 Corinthians 1:18 says: *"For the message of the cross is foolishness to those who are perishing, but to us who are being saved it is the power of God."* To say *"Yours is the power"* is to affirm that God's might is not only cosmic - it is personal. He uses His strength not to crush but to rescue, not to dominate but to deliver, not to control but to redeem.

This is a God who forgives, transforms, and restores. He pulls people out of spiritual death and breathes new life into them. That is true power.

Power to strengthen the weak

God's power is not only seen in creation and salvation - it is also available to strengthen His people. Isaiah gives us one of the most beloved promises in the Bible. It's found in Isaiah 40:29-31: *"He gives strength to the weary and increases the power of the weak. Even youths grow tired and weary, and young men stumble and fall; but those who hope in the Lord will renew their strength. They will soar on wings like eagles; they will run and not grow weary, they will walk and not be faint."*

This is not motivational poetry - it is spiritual reality. The power that raised Christ from the dead is available to you and me as we face the demands of life, the trials of faith, and the battles of the soul.

Ephesians 1:19–20 says: *"…his incomparably great power for us who believe. That power is the same as the mighty strength he exerted when he raised Christ from the dead…"* To say *"Yours is the power"* is to rest in the sufficiency of God when our strength runs out. It is a bold declaration of dependence - not weakness.

Power to overcome the enemy

We have already explored the reality of spiritual warfare and the prayer for deliverance from the evil one. The doxology now reminds us that the strength to fight does not come from us. Ephesians 6:10 says: *"Finally, be strong in the Lord and in his mighty power."*

Spiritual battles cannot be fought with human strategies. They require divine weapons and God-given strength. Too many Christians live in defeat not because the enemy is stronger, but because they are fighting alone. The power of God is our shield, our sword, and our victory.

When we pray *"Yours is the power,"* we are not merely praising - we are invoking divine strength for daily battle. Paul reminds us in 2 Corinthians 10:4, *"The weapons we fight with are not the weapons of the world. On the contrary, they have divine power to demolish strongholds."*

Power perfected in weakness

Perhaps the most paradoxical truth about God's power is that it is most fully displayed in our weakness. Paul pleaded with God to remove a thorn from his flesh - and God responded not with removal, but with grace: 2 Corinthians 12:9: *"But he said to me, 'My grace is sufficient for you, for my power is made perfect in weakness.' Therefore I will boast all the more gladly about my weaknesses, so that Christ's power may rest on me."*

This flips our understanding of strength upside down. In the world, weakness is shameful. In the Kingdom, weakness is the stage on which God displays His glory.

To say *"Yours is the power"* is to stop pretending we're strong and instead rely on the power of the indwelling Christ. It is to welcome God's strength into our fragile, fractured lives.

Power that releases holiness

The power of God is not just for miracles or external victories - it is also the power that transforms us from within. 2 Peter 1:3 declares: *"His divine power has given us everything we need for a godly life through our knowledge of him who called us by his own glory and goodness."*

We cannot produce holiness through self-effort. We are changed by grace-powered obedience - through the Spirit's work in us. The same power that saved us now sanctifies us. As we pray *"Yours is the power,"* we are actually saying, *"Lord, continue your transforming work in me. Make me holy. Make me whole. I cannot do this on my own."*

The phrase *"For yours is the power"* is more than a poetic ending - it is a life-altering truth. Every miracle, every answered prayer, every act of mercy, and every changed heart is a testimony to God's active power.

This part of the doxology invites us to surrender our illusion of control and to lean wholly on the One who alone has strength to save, to sanctify, and to sustain.

The meaning of glory

When we say, *"For yours is the glory,"* we are giving God what is rightly His: honour, praise, and recognition of His majesty. The Hebrew word for glory, *kabod,* carries the sense of weight or significance - something that is heavy with meaning, splendour, and worth. In the New Testament, the Greek word doxa conveys ideas of brilliance, honour, and divine radiance. God's glory is both His intrinsic nature and the recognition of that nature by His creation. He is glorious in essence - and when we worship, we are acknowledging that reality and proclaiming it back to Him.

Psalm 29:2 invites us: *"Ascribe to the Lord the glory due his name; worship the Lord in the splendour of his holiness."* Glory is not something we create or give to God in the sense of supplying it - it is something we recognize and respond to. We reflect it, we proclaim it, and we delight in it.

Glory seen in creation

The glory of God is revealed throughout His creation. The natural world is a canvas upon which the Creator has painted His splendour. Psalm 19:1 declares: *"The heavens declare the glory of God; the skies proclaim the work of his hands."* From the vast galaxies to the intricate design of a flower, every detail whispers of the glory of God.

Creation does not exist for its own sake - it exists to point us to the Creator. The world is not the main character; God is. Everything that exists does so to reflect His glory.

Romans 1:20 reinforces this: *"For since the creation of the world God's invisible qualities - his eternal power and divine nature - have been clearly seen, being understood from what has been made, so that people are without excuse."*

When we pray *"Yours is the glory,"* we join the song of creation and acknowledge the One whose fingerprint is on every mountain, every star, and every soul.

Glory displayed in redemption

While God's glory is evident in the natural world, it is most fully revealed in the person and work of Jesus Christ. The cross is the most paradoxical moment of glory in human history. There, Jesus was lifted up - not on a throne, but on a tree.

Yet in that moment of apparent defeat, God's justice, mercy, and love were on full display. John 1:14 tells us: *"The Word became flesh and made his dwelling among us. We have seen his glory, the glory of the one and only Son, who came from the Father, full of grace and truth."*

Jesus is the radiance of God's glory (Hebrews 1:3). In Him, the invisible God is made visible. In Him, the splendour of heaven entered the suffering of earth. In Him, the glory of God shines through human flesh, divine compassion, and also victorious resurrection. When we say, *"Yours is the glory,"* we are pointing to the cross and the empty tomb and saying, *"All honour belongs to You, Lord. You have done what no one else could do."*

Glory claimed by no other

God does not share His glory with anyone. This is not arrogance - it is the reality that there is no other being worthy of it. *"I am the Lord; that is my name! I will not yield my glory to another or my praise to idols."* (Isaiah 42:8).

To attempt to steal glory from God - whether through pride, self-exaltation, or idolatry - is to walk a dangerous path. The Bible consistently warns against taking credit for what God has done. In Acts 12, King Herod gave a public address and the crowd shouted, *"This is the voice of a god, not a man."* Because he did not give glory to God, Scripture says he was struck down and died.

Glory belongs to God alone. To say *"Yours is the glory"* is to step off the throne of self, reject applause that belongs to heaven, and to remember that we are servants, not stars - reflections, not the source.

Glory is the goal of all things

Everything in creation exists for one ultimate purpose: the glory of God. This includes our lives, our work, our worship, and even our trials. Romans 11:36 captures it powerfully: *"For from him and through him and for him are all things. To him be the glory forever! Amen."* This verse is not just theological - it is deeply practical. It means that everything we do should point others to God's worth. Our purpose in life is not self-fulfilment, but God-exaltation.

1 Corinthians 10:31 says: *"So whether you eat or drink or whatever you do, do it all for the glory of God."* This changes how we view everything. Our jobs become acts of worship. Our relationships become opportunities to reflect Jesus Christ. Even our suffering becomes a stage on which God's grace can shine. When we pray *"Yours is the glory,"* we are declaring: *"Lord, let every part of my life exist to make You known and honoured."*

Glory manifested in the Church

The Church is not just a gathering of believers - it is a vessel for God's glory. Ephesians 3:20–21: *"Now to him who is able to do immeasurably more than all we ask or imagine, according to his power that is at work within us, to him be glory in the church and in Christ Jesus throughout all generations, for ever and ever! Amen."*

The Church is called to reflect the character and purposes of God across the world. Our unity, our love, our worship, and our service are meant to shine a spotlight on the One who called us. The world should be able to look at the Church and say: *"There is something of God's glory among them."* When we pray *"Yours is the glory,"* we are committing ourselves to be a visible sign of God's invisible splendour -a living witness to His transforming power.

Glory that transforms us

Not only are we called to always glorify God - we are also being transformed by His glory. 2 Corinthians 3:18: *"And we all, who with unveiled faces contemplate the Lord's glory, are being transformed into his image with ever-increasing glory, which comes from the Lord, who is the Spirit."*

To gaze upon God's glory is to be changed by it. The more we behold His holiness, the more we become holy. The more we meditate on His majesty, the more our lives take on the shape of His Son. Glorifying God is not about merely singing louder or acting piously - it's about becoming more like Him. It's about allowing the Spirit to shape us into vessels that reflect His light.

Eternal glory awaits us

Finally, when we say *"Yours is the glory,"* we are looking forward to the day when God's glory will fill all things - when His radiance will no longer be veiled or resisted. Revelation 21:23 gives us a stunning picture of that day: *"The city does not need the sun or the moon to shine on it, for the glory of God gives it light, and the Lamb is its lamp."* In eternity, there will be no doubt about who reigns, who saves, who is worthy. The glory of God will be our light, our song, and our joy forever. Until then, we pray with longing, with faith, and with devotion: *"For yours is the kingdom and the power and the glory forever. Amen."*

Conclusion

This final phrase in the Lord's Prayer returns us to the very heart of it all - the glory of God. Everything we pray, everything we seek, everything we do is to be for His honour. We began The Lord's Prayer with: *"Our Father in heaven, hallowed be your name,"* and we end with: *"For yours is the glory."* It is a full-circle moment - from reverence to reliance, from confession to commission, and finally, to exaltation. As we pray this final line, let us not rush through it.

Let us let the weight of glory settle on our hearts and transform our perspective. Let us be people who live not for the applause of man, but for the honour of God.

To Him be the glory - now and forever.

12. 'AMEN'

The word that echoes eternity

It may be just one word, but it carries the weight of the entire prayer. Amen is not merely a religious sign-off, like a spiritual version of *"The End."* It's a response, a confession, and a firm commitment.

In the Bible, it is a word of strong affirmation and alignment. It declares, *"So be it!" or "Let it be true!"* or *"I agree!"* The word Amen comes from the Hebrew *'āmēn*, derived from a root that means to confirm, support, or be faithful.

In both the Old and New Testaments, it is used as a solemn affirmation of truth. When we pray *"Amen"* at the end of The Lord's Prayer, we are doing more than closing our eyes and preparing to move on. We are sealing our prayer with conviction. We are declaring: *"I believe this prayer. I trust this God. I commit to live in the light of these truths."*

Amen as a word of faith

To say *Amen* is to express faith - not in ourselves, but in the God to whom we have prayed. The entire prayer assumes that God is good, sovereign, wise, attentive, and able to respond. So when we say *Amen*, we are saying, *"Yes, I believe You are who You say You are. I believe You hear me. I believe You will act."*

Paul makes an astounding declaration in 2 Corinthians 1:20, *"For no matter how many promises God has made, they are 'Yes' in Christ. And so through him the 'Amen' is spoken by us to the glory of God."* Here, Paul tells us that Jesus is the fulfilment of every divine promise, and our Amen is a faith-filled echo of God's resounding Yes. We are not throwing hopeful words into the void - we are directing our prayers to a God who has already guaranteed His faithfulness through Christ.

Amen becomes the believer's way of saying: *"I take You at Your word. I trust You to answer as only You can."*

Amen as a word of surrender

Faith is not just mental agreement - it is trusting submission. So to say *Amen* is to surrender. It is to take our hands off the wheel and say, *"Lord, I have prayed as best I know how, but I leave the outcome with You."* Even Jesus, in the Garden of Gethsemane, modelled this attitude of surrendered prayer. Though He did not use the word *Amen* in that moment, He lived its truth: *"Yet not as I will, but as you will."* (Matthew 26:39). Every *Amen* is an echo of that posture. It says, *"I may not know how You will answer, but I trust that Your will is better than mine."* This is not passivity - it is active trust. It is saying, *"I won't try to force Your hand, Lord. I release my requests into Your capable hands."*

Amen as a word of agreement

Amen is not just for private prayers - it's also an very important communal affirmation. In Scripture, *Amen* was often spoken by a whole congregation in response to a declaration or blessing. Deuteronomy 27:15 and following includes a litany of laws and blessings, each followed by: *"Then all the people shall say, 'Amen!'"* In Nehemiah 8:6, after Ezra praised the Lord and read the Law, we read: *"And all the people lifted their hands and responded, 'Amen! Amen!' Then they bowed down and worshiped the Lord with their faces to the ground."* In the New Testament, we see similar affirmations in worship and teaching. Paul encouraged orderly worship in which people could say *"Amen"* to the prayers and prophecies shared (1 Corinthians 14:16). So when we say Amen aloud in church, we are not just participating in tradition - we are expressing unity. We are saying, *"Yes, I agree. I believe this too."* It is a way of linking hearts and faith across the body of Christ.

Amen as a word of resolve

To say Amen is not just a closing word - it is a launching pad. It is a resolve to live in the truth of what we've just prayed. Every line of the Lord's Prayer is a call to action:

➢ *"Hallowed be your name"* - then live to honour Him.
➢ *"Your kingdom come"* - then live as a citizen of His kingdom.

- ➤ *"Give us today our daily bread"* - then trust Him and practice contentment.
- ➤ *"Forgive us… as we forgive"* - then walk in both grace and grace-giving.
- ➤ *"Deliver us from the evil one"* - then walk in holiness and dependence.

The final *Amen* says: *"Lord, I don't want to just speak these words. I want to live them. I want my life to reflect the priorities of Your kingdom."* As James reminds us in James 1:22: *"Do not merely listen to the word and so deceive yourselves. Do what it says."* *Amen* is a commitment to obedience.

Amen and the character of Christ

Revelation 3:14 gives Jesus one of the most intriguing titles in Scripture: *"These are the words of the Amen, the faithful and true witness, the ruler of God's creation."* Jesus is not just the one who says Amen - He is the Amen. That is, He is the ultimate *'Yes'* to all of God's promises and purposes. He is the confirmation of God's truth, the fulfillment of God's mighty plan, and the living embodiment of God's will.

When we end The Lord's Prayer with *Amen*, we are doing more than concluding a prayer - we are fixing our eyes on the person of Christ. Our confidence is not in our eloquence, our effort, or even our faithfulness. It is in His. Our prayers reach the Father because they are carried by the Son. As the write of Hebrews says: *"Therefore he is able to save completely those who come to God through him, because he always lives to intercede for them."* (7:25). Jesus is the *Amen* to every prayer that seeks the Father's will. He is the final Word and the faithful Witness. He is the very reason we can say Amen with confidence.

So we come now to the end of The Lord's Prayer - but we do not come to the end of our praying, our trusting, or our living. Amen is a one-word chapter. It says: *"I believe. I trust. I agree. I surrender. I commit."* It is the resounding exclamation point of faith that sends us back into the world with confidence in God's rule, His power, and His glory.

Amen shapes our walk

The *Amen* at the end of the Lord's Prayer is not just the closing of a spiritual transaction - it is a bold declaration that shapes the way we live. It is the word that launches us back into the world with a deep, renewed awareness of God's truth and a fresh commitment to walk in it. Romans 12:1 urges us: *"Therefore, I urge you, brothers and sisters, in view of God's mercy, to offer your bodies as a living sacrifice, holy and pleasing to God - this is your true and proper worship."* Saying *Amen* is not the conclusion of our worship - it is its continuation. It's not the period at the end of a prayer but the beginning of a life lived in agreement with heaven. If The Lord's Prayer has truly taken root in our hearts, the Amen sends us out to live differently:

> ➤ If we have prayed for His name to be hallowed - we must honour Him with our speech, conduct, and values.
> ➤ If we have asked for His kingdom to come - we must align our priorities with His rule.
> ➤ If we've asked for forgiveness - we must extend it to others.
> ➤ If we've asked for deliverance from evil - we must reject sin and cling to holiness.

The *Amen* sends us back into daily life with a renewed posture of obedience, gratitude, and expectancy. It is the sacred *"Yes"* that turns prayer into practice.

Amen anchors us in assurance

In seasons when our prayers seem unanswered or our hearts are weary, the word *Amen* becomes a powerful anchor. It reminds us that even when we don't see immediate results, we can still trust in the character of God. The Psalms are filled with prayers that end in Amen, even when the psalmist is still waiting for deliverance or clarity. Psalm 41 concludes: *"Praise be to the Lord, the God of Israel, from everlasting to everlasting. Amen and Amen."* (Psalm 41:13). It's a double *Amen*, a way of reinforcing conviction even in the midst of struggle. The psalmist may still be waiting - but he is waiting with faith, grounded in the unchanging nature of our God.

There are times when saying *Amen* is an act of defiance against fear, doubt, or discouragement. It is saying, *"Lord, I don't yet see the answer - but I still believe. I still trust. I still affirm Your goodness."* This is echoed in Habakkuk 3:17-18: *"Though the fig tree does not bud and there are no grapes on the vines... yet I will rejoice in the Lord, I will be joyful in God my Saviour."* That is *Amen* in action - it is a faithful resolve to believe God's promises every day even when circumstances have not yet changed.

Amen helps us persevere in prayer

The word *Amen* reminds us that our prayers are a vital part of a relationship, not a ritual. They are not performance pieces or magic words, they are intimate conversations with our Father in heaven. And conversations continue. The *Amen* doesn't say, *"I'm done talking to You,"* but rather, *"I trust You enough to wait."* Luke 18:1 tells us: *"Then Jesus told his disciples a parable to show them that they should always pray and not give up."* The parable that follows - about the persistent widow - reminds us that prayer is not always answered immediately, but perseverance is powerful. *Amen* strengthens that perseverance.

Each time we conclude a prayer with this word *Amen*, we are recommitting to wait, to trust, and to come back again. Romans 12:12 exhorts us: *"Be joyful in hope, patient in affliction, faithful in prayer."* The word Amen fuels that faithfulness. It is not a signal to give up, but a stepping stone to the next prayer, and the next - until we either see the answer or see the Lord face to face.

Amen is the song of the saints

One of the most profound uses of Amen in Scripture is in the heavenly scenes of worship. In the Book of Revelation, the chorus of heaven includes this word again and again.

Revelation 7:11-12: *"All the angels were standing around the throne and around the elders and the four living creatures. They fell down on their faces before the throne and worshiped God, saying: 'Amen! Praise and glory and wisdom and thanks and honour and power and strength be to our God for ever and ever. Amen!'"*

This is not a quiet *Amen* whispered at the end of a prayer - this is a thunderous, cosmic affirmation of God's supremacy and God's eternal reign. This heavenly *Amen* reminds us that we are part of something far bigger than ourselves. Every time we say Amen, we are joining the eternal worship of the saints and angels. We are lifting our voice in harmony with heaven. We are saying, *"What You have done is worthy of praise. What You will do is worthy of trust. And who You are is worthy of glory."*

Amen and the assurance of salvation

Perhaps the most powerful Amen of all is the one spoken in response to the gospel. When a sinner hears the good news that Christ died for their sins, was raised to life, and offers forgiveness and eternal life - the only fitting response is: *"Amen! I believe it!"* Romans 10:9-10 tells us: *"If you declare with your mouth, 'Jesus is Lord,' and believe in your heart that God raised him from the dead, you will be saved. For it is with your heart that you believe and are justified, and it is with your mouth that you profess your faith and are saved."*

That confession is the ultimate *Amen*. It is the soul's agreement with heaven's truth. It is saying, *"Yes, Lord - I believe. I receive. I surrender."* Every time we say Amen, we are reminded of the great 'Yes' we gave to Jesus when we first believed. And we are called to keep living in the light of that Amen - each and every day.

Amen and the mission of Christ

Finally, Amen propels us into mission. The Lord's Prayer does not end in resignation - it actually ends in exclamation. Amen is not a sigh; it is a call to action.

When we say *Amen* to *"Your kingdom come,"* we must also go and proclaim that kingdom. When we say *Amen* to *"Forgive us our sins,"* we must go and extend forgiveness. When we say *Amen* to *"Deliver us from the evil one,"* we must go then and resist temptation, empowered by the Spirit. Our lives become an *Amen* to God's purposes - a visible, audible, tangible expression of what we've prayed.

Jesus said in John 20:21: *"As the Father has sent me, I am sending you."* And in Matthew 28:19: *"Therefore go and make disciples of all nations…"* We cannot say *Amen* to the Lord's Prayer and remain idle. The Amen sends us out - with the gospel on our lips and the love of Christ in our hands. It pushes us beyond the church pew and into the streets, classrooms, offices, and homes - to live what we have prayed.

The word *Amen* is so much more than a ancient tradition. It is a bold, loud, declaration of faith, a posture of trust, a commitment to obedience, and a joining in the worship of heaven. It anchors us in hard times, fuels our perseverance, and launches us into the mission of God. It is both the final word of the prayer and the first step of our response.

As we move to the final part of this book, we will look at *Amen* as a prophetic word - a glimpse into eternity, and a bold, daily confession of faith in a world that often tempts us to doubt. Let us be a people who not only pray *Amen*, but who live *Amen* - with hearts that trust, mouths that praise, and lives that reflect the Kingdom we long for.

Amen as a prophetic declaration

When we say *Amen* at the end of the Lord's Prayer, we are not simply concluding a conversation with God - we are proclaiming a future reality. We are declaring that everything we have prayed for will one day be fully, finally, and gloriously fulfilled. The kingdom will come. God's will shall be done on earth as it is in heaven. Daily needs will no longer exist, because we will feast in the presence of the Lamb. Forgiveness will be fully realised, and temptation and evil will be banished forever.

When we say Amen, we are saying, *"Yes, Lord - I believe Your future is secure, Your promises are sure, and Your victory is final."* In this sense, Amen is a word of holy expectation. It points us forward to what is coming, even when our present moment is hard. In Revelation 22:20, the final words of in the Bible say: *"He who testifies to these things says, 'Yes, I am coming soon.' Amen. Come, Lord Jesus."*

Here, *Amen* is an exclamation of longing - the heart's deep cry for Christ's return and the completion of God's redemptive plan. Every time we pray *Amen*, we are echoing that same desire, which is always: "*Come, Lord Jesus.*"

Amen and the certainty of God's promises

The word *Amen* is not built on wishful thinking. It is grounded in the unshakeable certainty of God's faithfulness. That's what makes it prophetic - it speaks the truth of God's promises before they are visible. Numbers 23:19 declares: "*God is not human, that he should lie, not a human being, that he should change his mind. Does he speak and then not act? Does he promise and not fulfill?*"

When we say *Amen*, we are aligning ourselves with this truth. We are trusting that what God has said, He will do. That the kingdom we pray for will come. That the enemy we resist will be defeated. That the glory we affirm belongs to God forever. This is not naive optimism. It is actually spiritual realism - faith that is rooted in the character of a faithful God.

Romans 8:24-25 gives voice to this kind of trust: "*For in this hope we were saved. But hope that is seen is no hope at all. Who hopes for what they already have? But if we hope for what we do not yet have, we wait for it patiently.*" *Amen* is the believer's patient hope made vocal. It is our verbal stand on the promises of God, even when we don't see them yet.

Amen and the worship of Heaven

The Book of Revelation presents us with a chorus of *Amens* that reverberate throughout all of heaven. These *Amens* are not just affirmations - they are acts of worship. They are the heavenly response to the glory of God, the triumph of Christ, and the unfolding of God's eternal plan. Revelation 5:13-14 offers one such scene: "*Then I heard every creature in heaven and on earth and under the earth and on the sea, and all that is in them, saying: 'To him who sits on the throne and to the Lamb be praise and honour and glory and power, for ever and ever!' The four living creatures said, 'Amen,' and the elders fell down and worshiped.*"

What a breathtaking picture we have there - all creation declaring the supremacy of Christ, followed by *Amen*, and then worship that goes beyond words. When we say *Amen*, we are rehearsing for eternity. We are really aligning ourselves with the worship of heaven, the praise of angels, and the joy of redeemed saints who see the Lamb on the throne and know that all is well.

Amen and the courage to keep going

Life is often marked by struggle, confusion, pain, and waiting. There are times when praying the Lord's Prayer feels easy and other times when every word feels costly. In those moments, *Amen* becomes a word of courage. It takes courage to say Amen when:

> ➤ Your prayers feel unanswered
> ➤ Your heart is heavy with grief
> ➤ Your future feels uncertain
> ➤ Your faith feels fragile

But this is where the real power of *Amen* can be found - not in the absence of struggle, but in the presence of trust. Hebrews 10:23 exhorts us: *"Let us hold unswervingly to the hope we profess, for he who promised is faithful."* *Amen* is the sound of holding on. It is the voice of hope refusing to let go. It is the declaration that, even in the depth of the valley, we believe in the mountaintop promises of God. When we pray *Amen* at the end of The Lord's Prayer, we are not escaping our trials -we are bringing them to the throne of grace and trusting the One who reigns above them.

Amen and the Church's testimony

The early church adopted *Amen* as a word of confession and conviction. It was spoken during baptisms, at the Lord's Supper, during preaching, and in prayer. It was a way of bearing witness to the truth and standing with all our fellow believers. In many congregations today, *Amen* is still spoken aloud - and for very good reason. It is not just a ritual - it is a communal declaration: *"We believe this. We agree. We will live this."*

It strengthens unity, affirms truth, and calls the whole body to action. 1 Timothy 1:17 captures this spirit of corporate worship: *"Now to the King eternal, immortal, invisible, the only God, be honour and glory for ever and ever. Amen."*

When the church says *Amen*, we are declaring that God alone deserves all our worship, all allegiance, and all glory. It's a countercultural confession in a world that glorifies self. It's a bold stand in a culture that often mocks faith. It's a public act of agreement with the will and the purposes of God.

Amen as the final word

As we come to the close of The Lord's Prayer, the word *Amen* reminds us that all things are ultimately heading toward God. History, prayer, mission, worship, and eternity all find their end in Him.

Paul says it best in Romans 11:36: *"For from him and through him and for him are all things. To him be the glory forever! Amen."* That is the ultimate reality. That is the note that rings through eternity. That is the truth that undergirds every prayer, every chapter, every life surrendered to Jesus.

The *Amen* of The Lord's Prayer is not just the end of the prayer - it is the believer's daily *"Yes"* to everything God is, everything God has done, and everything God will do.

Conclusion

The Lord's Prayer ends as it began - with a focus on God, not us.

➢ It begins with *"Our Father in heaven"* - a reminder of His nearness and majesty.
➢ It ends with *"Amen"* - a bold declaration of our trust in His reign, power, and glory.

To really live an *Amen* life is to live in perpetual agreement with heaven. It is to wake up each day and say:

> ➤ *"Yes, Lord - Your name be hallowed …"*

> ➤ *"Yes, Lord - Your kingdom come …"*

> ➤ *"Yes, Lord - Your will be done …"*

> ➤ *"Yes, Lord - provide for me, forgive me, lead me, and deliver me …"*

> ➤ *"Yes, Lord - Yours is the kingdom, the power, and the glory. Amen."*

Let this final word of The Lord's Prayer become the first word of your next steps. Let it resound not just from your lips, but from your heart and your life. Because *Amen* is not just how we end a prayer - it's how we live a prayer!

13. 'LIVING A LIFE OF PRAYER'

From routine to relationship

For twelve chapters, we have journeyed through the words of Jesus in The Lord's Prayer - a divine blueprint that teaches us how to speak with God, how to align our hearts with His will, and how to find rest in His presence. But now we must take the next step - not simply learning to say our prayers, but to live a life of prayer.

The Lord's Prayer is not just something to be recited; it is something to be absorbed and embodied. It calls us into a rhythm of communion with God that shapes every part of life - not just our Sundays or our morning devotions, but our relationships, our work, our thoughts, and even our reactions. Prayer is not a moment in time; it is a way of life.

That is what the Paul is speaking about in these three short verses, which form one of the clearest descriptions of the prayer-saturated life in the entire Bible. Paul writes: *"Rejoice always, pray continually, give thanks in all circumstances; for this is God's will for you in Christ Jesus."* (1 Thessalonians 5:16-18). Here we see prayer not as an occasional discipline, but as the heartbeat of a life grounded in Christ.

"Pray continually" – A new vision for prayer

The phrase *"pray continually"* does not mean we have to spend every moment on our knees or speak aloud to God all day long. Rather, Paul is painting a picture of ongoing communion - an awareness of God's presence that undergirds everything we do. To pray continually is to actually live in a constant posture of dependence, trust, and spiritual attentiveness. It is to keep the door to heaven open, the line of communication unbroken. It is to carry the presence of God into every conversation, every decision, and every challenge. This kind of prayer life does not wait for quiet times or special occasions. It flows through our day like breath - not always formal or eloquent, but real and present.

Brother Lawrence, the 17th-century monk who wrote *The Practice of the Presence of God,* described prayer as simply being aware of God's nearness in every task: *"There is not in the world a kind of life more sweet and delightful than that of a continual conversation with God."* This is what it really looks like to live the prayer life. It's not compartmentalised – it's just continual. Not limited to our devotions but integrated into our whole existence.

Jesus modelled a life of prayer

The Lord's Prayer is just one glimpse into the relationship Jesus had with the Father. His entire life was bathed in prayer. From the desert to the mountainside, from early mornings to lonely nights, Jesus constantly retreated to pray and seek communion with His Father. Luke 5:16 tells us: *"But Jesus often withdrew to lonely places and prayed."*

Before choosing the twelve disciples, He spent the whole night in prayer (Luke 6:12). Before His greatest trial in Gethsemane, He poured out His heart in agony to His Father (Luke 22:44). He prayed before feeding the crowds, before raising the dead, and even while dying on the cross. Jesus didn't just pray occasionally. He lived in prayer. It wasn't simply a tool for crisis moments - it was the foundation of His life. If the Son of God needed to pray continually, how much more do we?

From duty to delight

One reason many believers struggle to pray continually is that prayer feels like a duty rather than a delight. We see it as a box to tick - one more spiritual task among many. But that is not how Scripture describes prayer. Psalm 16:11 says: *"You make known to me the path of life; you will fill me with joy in your presence, with eternal pleasures at your right hand."*

Prayer is not about fulfilling religious obligations - it is about entering into joy, the joy of being known and loved by God. To live a life of prayer is to learn to enjoy God's company. It is to speak with Him as you would with a beloved friend - not always asking for things but just being with Him.

When we shift our mindset from obligation to relationship, prayer will become a great source of strength, comfort, guidance, and renewal.

Rejoice always, pray continually, give thanks

Paul doesn't just say pray continually. He sandwiches it between two other imperatives: *"Rejoice always"* and *"Give thanks in all circumstances."* These three commands form a trio of grace that together define the life of faith.

➤ *Rejoice always* - not because everything is good, but because God is good.

➤ *Pray continually* - because life apart from God is dry and anxious.

➤ *Give thanks* - because gratitude anchors our hearts in His faithfulness.

This is a pattern of spiritual resilience. These words were written to a church under pressure and persecution. Paul wasn't offering a simplistic formula - he was describing the fuel that would keep their faith burning in the face of difficulty. To pray continually is to keep ourselves aligned with the reality of God's presence, no matter what we are walking through.

Developing a lifestyle of prayer

So how do we do this? How do we move from those occasional moments of prayer to a continual life of prayer? Here are four practical ways to develop a prayer-saturated life:

a) *Begin and end with God:* Start your day by acknowledging Him - even before your feet hit the floor. Thank Him for breath, ask Him for wisdom, and surrender the day ahead. End your day in prayer - reflecting, repenting, rejoicing.

b) *Make prayer your first response, not a last Resort:* When you feel anxious, pray. When you feel tempted, pray. When you see beauty, pray. When you hear bad news, pray. Train your heart to turn to God immediately and instinctively.

c) Turn everyday moments into prayer: Driving in your car? Thank God for His protection. Waiting in line? Pray for the person in front of you. Washing dishes? Pray for a clean heart. Let prayer permeate the ordinary.

d) Use Scripture as fuel for prayer: Let God's Word shape your words. As you read the Bible, turn it into prayer. If you read, *"The Lord is my shepherd,"* respond with: *"Lord, lead me today. I need You."*

This is God's will for you

Paul ends with a powerful reminder: *"For this is God's will for you in Christ Jesus."* So often, we ask, *"What is God's will for my life?"* And here it is - clear, simple, and direct: Rejoice. Pray. Give thanks. God's will is not only about what career we pursue or what city we live in. It's about how we walk with Him in the present moment.

A life of rejoicing, praying, and gratitude is a life fully aligned with God's desires for us. Prayer isn't just for spiritual elites or pastors. It's God's will for every believer. In this chapter we are moving from the words of the Lord's Prayer into the way of life that those words invite us into. To live a life of prayer:

➤ Remain in constant fellowship with our heavenly Father
➤ Draw strength and joy from His presence
➤ Anchor ourselves in His promises
➤ Walk through every moment with hearts tuned to His voice

Let us move beyond viewing prayer as a duty. Let us enter into it as a delight, a daily rhythm, and a lifelong pursuit. And let the Lord's Prayer not only shape our prayers - but shape our lives.

Real life demands real prayer

Living a life of prayer means we do not retreat from reality - we bring prayer into reality. It means we are honest about our fears, our needs, and our pressures, but we don't carry them alone. We carry them to the Father.

Philippians 4:4-7 *"Rejoice in the Lord always. I will say it again: Rejoice! Let your gentleness be evident to all. The Lord is near. Do not be anxious about anything, but in every situation, by prayer and petition, with thanksgiving, present your requests to God. And the peace of God, which transcends all understanding, will guard your hearts and your minds in Christ Jesus."*

Paul speaks into the real world - a world of stress, anxiety, and relational tension. He does not call for denial or spiritual escapism. Instead, he gives us a rhythm for living that includes hardship but keeps us rooted in divine peace. We are told to rejoice always, not to be anxious about anything, and in every situation, by prayer and petition, with thanksgiving, to present our requests to God. That's what a life of prayer looks like - prayerful realism grounded in the nearness of God.

"The Lord is near" - The foundation of prayerful living

The call to rejoice, pray, and release anxiety is not based on willpower. It's based on a profound truth: *"The Lord is near."* This nearness is not metaphorical or emotional - it is real, immediate, and powerful.

In Christ, God has come close. Through the Spirit, He abides in us. The veil has been torn. Heaven is no longer distant. This is why we can pray in the midst of any circumstance - because God is right there in the middle of it.

Jesus promised in John 14:23: *"Anyone who loves me will obey my teaching. My Father will love them, and we will come to them and make our home with them."* God does not just visit us occasionally. He makes His home with us. This is the foundation of continual prayer - the permanent presence of a faithful God.

Turning anxiety into prayer

Paul's words in Philippians 4:6 are among the most practical and powerful teachings on prayer in all of Scripture: *"Do not be anxious about anything, but in every situation, by prayer and petition, with thanksgiving, present your requests to God."*

Notice the contrast here:

➤ Anxiety happens when we internalize our fears, carry burdens alone, and imagine worst-case scenarios.

➤ Prayer happens when we externalize those fears, give them to God, and trust Him with the outcome.

Paul doesn't say *"don't feel anxious"* - he says, *"when you feel anxious, don't hold on to it. Turn it into prayer."* Take the same energy, the same focus, the same passion - and redirect it into communion with God. This is one of the most transformational habits of the Christian life: whenever anxiety knocks, answer it with prayer.

Present your requests - all of them

Paul says we should present our requests to God in all situations. There is nothing which is too small, too big, too mundane, or too complicated. Prayer is not reserved for crises or holy moments. God invites us to bring every concern before Him - from grocery bills to global issues, from parenting struggles to career moves, from grief to gratitude. Colossians 4:2 says: *"Devote yourselves to prayer, being watchful and thankful."* This verse captures three powerful habits:

➤ *Devotion* - make prayer a priority, not an afterthought.
➤ *Watchfulness* - stay spiritually alert, noticing God's hand in the world.
➤ *Thankfulness* - ground your prayer in remembrance of God's faithfulness.

When we present all our requests with these three attitudes in mind, prayer becomes more than reaction - it becomes revelation. We begin to see the world through God's eyes, not just ours.

The power of thanksgiving in prayer

It's easy to overlook this detail, but Paul insists that our prayers be accompanied with thanksgiving. Why? Because thanksgiving aligns our hearts with truth.

It reminds us of God's faithfulness in the past, which then gives us confidence for the future. When we thank God while we pray - not just after He answers -we're making a bold faith statement: *"I trust You even before the outcome."*

Thanksgiving in prayer changes the tone of our conversation with God. Instead of desperate pleading, we begin to speak with confidence. Instead of panic, we practice praise. Psalm 100:4 declares: *"Enter his gates with thanksgiving and his courts with praise; give thanks to him and praise his name."* Thanksgiving is the gateway to prayer. It opens our hearts and reminds us that we are speaking not to a reluctant deity, but to a loving Father.

The result: Peace that guards

Paul ends with a promise: *"And the peace of God, which transcends all understanding, will guard your hearts and your minds in Christ Jesus."* This is not merely emotional calm - it is supernatural peace that protects. Paul uses a military word here - *"guard"* - implying active defence. When we live a life of prayer, peace stands guard over our hearts (our emotions) and our minds (our thoughts). This is not peace because everything is perfect - it's peace in the midst of the imperfect.

Jesus offered this same kind of peace in John 14:27: *"Peace I leave with you; my peace I give you. I do not give to you as the world gives. Do not let your hearts be troubled and do not be afraid."* This peace is not the absence of trouble - it is the presence of Christ.

The practice of 'every situation' prayer

Let's look at what this kind of prayer might look like in everyday life.

➤ *Waking up:* "Lord, thank You for this day. Go before me."
➤ *Before a meeting:* "Holy Spirit, give me wisdom and peace."
➤ *In conflict:* "Father, help me to be patient and gentle."
➤ *During success:* "Thank You, Lord. All good things come from You."

- *During stress:* "I cast my cares on You, for You care for me."
- *While walking or driving:* "Lead me, Lord, and open my eyes."
- *While with family:* "Help me love well and listen carefully."
- *At the end of the day:* "Thank You for sustaining me. Forgive my failures. I rest in Your grace."

This is not about adding hours of formal prayer. It's about threading your day with divine awareness - making room for God in all things. Prayer is joyful communion with God, but it is also a practical necessity for navigating real life. Paul does not say, *"Pray when it's easy."* He says, *"Pray in every situation."* That includes:

- When you're tired
- When you're anxious
- When you're unsure
- When you're frustrated
- When you're joyful
- When you're grieving

There is no moment in life where prayer is inappropriate or ineffective. God invites us to bring it all to Him. Let us become the kind of people who do not just say prayers - but who live prayerfully. Who trust God enough to bring Him every situation. Who carry an atmosphere of heaven into the complexities of life on earth.

Prayer as relational formation

Prayer is not a solitary exercise for private benefit - it is deeply relational. When we live a life of prayer, it inevitably transforms how we live with others. The closer we draw to God in prayer, the more we reflect His heart in our relationships. The Lord's Prayer taught us to say, *"Forgive us our sins, as we forgive those who sin against us."* In that phrase alone, we saw that prayer is not only vertical (between us and God), but horizontal (between us and others).

Genuine prayer leads us into community, not away from it. It softens our hearts, removes bitterness, builds empathy, and ignites love. The prayer-filled life is the fertile soil where grace, patience, humility, and forgiveness grow - not because we try harder, but because we live in the very presence of the One Who models these things perfectly.

Prayer and reconciliation

Jesus made it clear that unresolved conflict hinders not only relationships but also our worship and prayer life. He said: *"Therefore, if you are offering your gift at the altar and there remember that your brother or sister has something against you, leave your gift there in front of the altar. First go and be reconciled to them; then come and offer your gift."* (Matthew 5:23–24)

This is radical. Jesus is saying that right relationships matter so much that God would rather we delay our religious offering than persist in unreconciled conflict. Why? Because God is not only interested in our devotion – He is interested in our integrity.

Prayer is not a hiding place from relational tension; it is a training ground for reconciliation. As we draw near to God in prayer, we are often convicted to draw near to others in grace. If we truly live a life of prayer, we will become peacemakers, not peace-fakers or peace-breakers.

Confession and healing in community

James 5:16 reveals another layer of relational prayer: *"Therefore confess your sins to each other and pray for each other so that you may be healed. The prayer of a righteous person is powerful and effective."* Prayer is not just about asking God for things; it includes confessing, listening, interceding, and healing - together.

This is one of the great weaknesses in modern Christian life: we have turned prayer into a solitary act, when the New Testament paints it as a communal one. In the early church, believers prayed together, confessed together, and were healed together.

When we begin to live a life of prayer, we become safe places for others to confess their sins, share their burdens, and receive healing. Prayer creates the spiritual atmosphere in which honesty and grace can flourish.

Prayer empowers forgiveness

Forgiveness is one of the most difficult acts of obedience - and one of the most powerful outcomes of a praying life. When we pray for someone who has hurt us, something supernatural begins to happen. Our pain doesn't disappear immediately, but our perspective shifts. We begin to see them through God's eyes, not just through the lens of our wounds.

In Matthew 5:44, Jesus said: *"But I tell you, love your enemies and pray for those who persecute you."* This is impossible apart from the grace of God - but prayer is the path by which that grace flows into our lives. We cannot hate those we consistently pray for. Living a life of prayer means asking God to do heart surgery in us - removing bitterness, resentment, and judgment, and then replacing it with love, understanding, and compassion.

Clothing ourselves in love through prayer

Paul describes the kind of character that flows out of a life immersed in prayer: *"Therefore, as God's chosen people, holy and dearly loved, clothe yourselves with compassion, kindness, humility, gentleness and patience. Bear with each other and forgive one another if any of you has a grievance against someone. Forgive as the Lord forgave you. And over all these virtues put on love, which binds them all together in perfect unity."* (Colossians 3:12-14)

This is the natural fruit of living in communion with Christ. A prayer-filled heart becomes a love-filled life. These qualities are not produced by effort alone, but by abiding in Christ. And prayer is that abiding - that continual connection to the vine that bears fruit.

Just as we put on physical clothes each day, so too we must clothe ourselves with Christlike virtues through daily communion with Him in prayer.

Praying for others: Intercession as love in action

When we pray for others, we participate in God's work in their lives. Intercessory prayer is not just spiritual activity - it is love in action. Paul modelled this kind of prayer constantly.

To the Colossians: *"We continually ask God to fill you with the knowledge of his will through all the wisdom and understanding that the Spirit gives..."* (Colossians 1:9).

To the Thessalonians: *"We always thank God for all of you and continually mention you in our prayers."* (1 Thessalonians 1:2)

To the Ephesians: *"I keep asking that the God of our Lord Jesus Christ, the glorious Father, may give you the Spirit of wisdom and revelation..."* (Ephesians 1:17)

Paul's letters are soaked in prayer for others. His theology was rich, but his intercession was relentless. When we live a life of prayer, we become priests, standing between others and God, lifting them up, carrying their burdens, and celebrating their growth.

Prayer and listening: Becoming a non-anxious presence

One of the most powerful ways prayer shapes our relationships is by teaching us to listen - not only to God, but to people. Prayer slows us down. It softens us. It trains our ears to hear the still small voice - and that same attentiveness flows into how we listen to others. In a world that rushes to speak, react, and judge, a praying person becomes a non-anxious presence - someone who listens deeply, responds gently, and remains grounded. The more time we spend in God's presence, the more present we become with others.

From isolation to interconnection

The modern world is deeply fragmented. People are lonely, distracted, and disconnected. But a community of people who live prayerfully - who love well, forgive freely, listen deeply, and intercede faithfully - becomes a healing force in the world.

This is what the church is meant to be: a praying people who become a living witness to the love, patience, and mercy of God. Prayer is not an escape from people - it is the empowerment to love them well.

Conclusion: Prayer is the furnace of transformation

When we began this chapter book, we entered the Lord's Prayer line by line. Now, as we explore the wider implications of prayer, we are discovering that prayer transforms everything - not just our relationship with God, but our relationship with others. Living a life of prayer:

➢ Softens our hearts toward others
➢ Breaks down walls of bitterness
➢ Cultivates grace, humility, and compassion
➢ Strengthens the bonds of unity
➢ Equips us to be peacemakers, forgivers, encouragers, and intercessors

As you pray, people will frustrate you less and inspire you more. Their faults will seem smaller, their burdens heavier, their humanity clearer. That is what happens when we see them as God sees them.

Let us become a people whose lives are soaked in prayer - not just in words, but in character, in relationship, in community. And let our churches become places where prayer is not merely heard in services - but felt in every relationship.

14. 'THE HOLY SPIRIT AND PRAYER'

In the previous chapter, we explored what it means to live a life of prayer - to commune with God in every situation, to pray without ceasing, and to always allow our relationship with Him to overflow into our relationships with others. But in order to sustain this kind of life, we must recognize that we are not left to do it in our own strength. God has given us a Helper - the Holy Spirit - to empower and sustain us in prayer.

Many Christians struggle with prayer because they believe it depends entirely on their own discipline, knowledge, or ability to articulate the right words. But Scripture tells us that the Spirit Himself helps us. He is not only present in our prayer - He is active in it. When we are weak, He is strong. When we are silent, He speaks. When we are confused, He brings clarity. In this chapter, we will explore how the Holy Spirit enables us to pray, intercedes for us, aligns us with the will of God, and teaches us to approach God as our loving Father.

The Spirit helps us in our weakness

Let us begin with Paul's letter to the Romans, one of the most profound texts on the Spirit's role in prayer: *"In the same way, the Spirit helps us in our weakness. We do not know what we ought to pray for, but the Spirit himself intercedes for us through wordless groans. And he who searches our hearts knows the mind of the Spirit, because the Spirit intercedes for God's people in accordance with the will of God."* (Romans 8:26-27).

This passage reminds us of two key truths: First, we are weak, and second, we are not alone. There are many times when we simply don't know what to say in prayer. We feel overwhelmed, confused, burdened, or exhausted. Paul is saying that in those moments, the Holy Spirit steps in. He does not abandon us - He intercedes with groanings too deep for words.

These are not incoherent cries. They are deeply spiritual expressions of our hearts' longing - brought before the Father by the Spirit, even when our minds can't form the right words.

What a comfort to know that the Spirit is not a passive observer in our prayers - He is an active participant.

The Spirit aligns our hearts with God's will

Paul also tells us in Romans 8:27 that the Spirit *"intercedes for God's people in accordance with the will of God."* That is a vital truth. Often, our prayers are driven by emotion, fear, or desire. We may ask for things that seem good to us but are not aligned with God's perfect will. The Spirit corrects and refines our prayers as they rise before the Father.

This means that even when we pray imperfectly, we can be confident that the Spirit is translating our prayers into the language of God's purposes. He shapes our desires, purifies our motives, and steers our hearts toward divine alignment. This doesn't mean we shouldn't pray boldly or honestly - far from it. God wants our raw prayers. But we can trust that the Holy Spirit is working even in our inarticulate or misdirected prayers to bring about God's best for us.

The Spirit bears witness that we are children of God

Another important passage is found in Romans 8:15-16: *"The Spirit you received does not make you slaves, so that you live in fear again; rather, the Spirit you received brought about your adoption to sonship. And by him we cry, 'Abba, Father.' The Spirit himself testifies with our spirit that we are God's children."*

This is not just theological information - it is genuine relational transformation. The Spirit teaches us to approach God not as a distant deity but as a loving Father. That word Abba is the Aramaic word for *"Daddy"* - intimate, warm, trusting. Without the Holy Spirit, prayer becomes formal, fearful, or distant. But with the Spirit, prayer becomes familial. We are not grovelling servants - we are beloved sons and daughters.

This identity changes everything. It gives us confidence, security, and peace in prayer. We don't need to manipulate or impress God. We come as children - welcomed, wanted, heard.

Jesus promised the Spirit would help us to pray

Before His death, Jesus promised that the Father would send another Helper - the Holy Spirit - to be with us forever: *"And I will ask the Father, and he will give you another advocate to help you and be with you forever - the Spirit of truth. The world cannot accept him, because it neither sees him nor knows him. But you know him, for he lives with you and will be in you."* (John 14:16–17)

Jesus was preparing His disciples for the time when He would no longer walk beside them physically - but He assured them they would not be abandoned. The Spirit would take His place, not merely beside them but within them. This promise is for us, too. We are never alone in prayer. The Spirit is our Advocate - which means one who comes alongside to help. He knows the Father perfectly. He knows us completely; He bridges the gap between our finite understanding and God's infinite wisdom.

Praying in the Spirit

Ephesians 6:18 gives us this instruction: *"And pray in the Spirit on all occasions with all kinds of prayers and requests. With this in mind, be alert and always keep on praying for all the Lord's people."* What does it mean to pray in the Spirit? It means to pray under the Spirit's influence, in His power, and in accordance with His leading. It means letting the Spirit guide our hearts, shape our words, direct our focus, and inspire our faith.

This can happen in structured prayers, spontaneous prayers, corporate prayers, and quiet personal prayers. It's not about volume or emotion - it's about dependence and a sensitivity to the Holy Spirit's presence. Praying in the Spirit is a posture of humility and surrender. It's a way of saying, *"Holy Spirit, lead me as I pray. Speak through me. Intercede for me. Align me with the Father's will."*

We do not know how to pray as we ought - and that's okay

So many Christians live under a burden of guilt about their prayer lives. They feel they're not eloquent enough, not faithful enough, not spiritual enough.

But Romans 8:26 offers great freedom: *"We do not know what we ought to pray for..."* Even Paul, writing to the Roman church, admits that we often don't know how to pray properly - and that's okay. That's not a reason to avoid prayer. It's a reason to lean more deeply on the Spirit. The Holy Spirit is not hindered by our ignorance. He meets us in our weakness and helps us express what we cannot articulate. The power of prayer is not in our words - it's in God's Spirit.

The Spirit is our prayer partner

We are not left to pray alone. The Holy Spirit is our guide, our advocate, our intercessor, and our helper. He draws us close to the Father, aligns our hearts with heaven, and enables us to pray beyond our limitations. In moments of joy, the Spirit inspires praise. In moments of sorrow, the Spirit gives us comfort. In moments of confusion, the Spirit brings clarity. In moments of silence, the Spirit speaks on our behalf. To live a life of prayer is not to master a certain technique - it is to cultivate a Spirit-filled relationship with the Father through the Son.

As we continue in this book, we will go deeper into what it means to walk by the Spirit, pray in the Spirit, and keep in step with the Spirit. But for now, just rest in this beautiful truth: You are never alone in prayer. The Spirit is praying with you, for you, and through you.

Prayer is a Spirit-led journey

The profound truth is that the Holy Spirit is not just present in our prayers - He is our helper, intercessor, and guide. Prayer is not meant to be a task we perform in our own strength. It is a Spirit-enabled relationship rooted in trust, adoption, and divine assistance.

Now, we turn our attention to a deeper question: How do we live a life of prayer that is consistently led by the Holy Spirit? What does it mean to *"keep in step with the Spirit,"* especially when it comes to prayer? The Christian life is not just about occasional moments of inspiration - it's about daily, Spirit-filled alignment.

As Paul wrote to the Galatians, *"Since we live by the Spirit, let us keep in step with the Spirit."* (Galatians 5:25). This is true in every aspect of our spiritual life - and especially true in our prayer life.

The Spirit-led life is the foundation of Spirit-led prayer

Let's begin with Galatians 5:16-18: *"So I say, walk by the Spirit, and you will not gratify the desires of the flesh. For the flesh desires what is contrary to the Spirit, and the Spirit what is contrary to the flesh. They are in conflict with each other, so that you are not to do whatever you want. But if you are led by the Spirit, you are not under the law."* Paul describes the internal conflict we all face: the desires of the flesh pull us in one direction, while the Spirit calls us in another. This battle plays out in many areas, including how we pray.

If our hearts are dominated by fear, selfishness, or pride, our prayers will reflect that. But when we *"walk by the Spirit,"* our prayers begin to reflect God's heart. We ask for things that align with His will. We become less reactive and more reflective. Our communion with God deepens, and our prayers become participation in His purposes, not just requests for our preferences.

Bearing the fruit of the Spirit through prayer

In Galatians 5:22-23, Paul famously lists the fruit of the Spirit: *"But the fruit of the Spirit is love, joy, peace, forbearance, kindness, goodness, faithfulness, gentleness and self-control."* These are not personality traits or moral goals - they are the natural outflow of living in step with the Spirit. And the key is connection: prayer is both a source and a setting where this fruit grows.

➤ As we pray, the Spirit cultivates love in us - not just for God, but for others.
➤ As we pray, joy begins to rise - even in suffering.
➤ As we pray, peace guards our hearts - just as Paul promised in Philippians 4.
➤ As we pray, patience is formed - we wait on God's timing, not our own.

➤ As we pray, kindness and gentleness grow - even toward our enemies.

➤ As we pray, self-control strengthens - helping us resist temptation.

A Spirit-led prayer life produces a Spirit-filled character. And the more our character reflects Christ, the more our prayers are aligned with His heart.

Building ourselves up in the Spirit

Jude 1:20 gives us a simple but powerful instruction: *"But you, dear friends, by building yourselves up in your most holy faith and praying in the Holy Spirit..."* To *"pray in the Holy Spirit"* is to lean into divine strength and spiritual wisdom - to allow the Spirit to form our prayers, fuel our faith, and focus our vision.

Jude's phrase *"building yourselves up"* would suggest something which is intentional and active. Prayer is not passive. It is how we strengthen our inner person. It is how we re-centre on truth. It is how we prepare ourselves for the trials and temptations of life. When we pray in the Spirit, we are not merely asking for things - we are being formed, fortified, and filled.

The Spirit leads us into Truth

Jesus promised His disciples that the Holy Spirit would be their teacher: *"But when he, the Spirit of truth, comes, he will guide you into all the truth. He will not speak on his own; he will speak only what he hears, and he will tell you what is yet to come."* (John 16:13). This is one of the most essential roles of the Spirit in our prayer lives.

As we pray, the Spirit leads us into truth - not just theological facts, but personal revelation. He shows us where we are holding on to lies. He convicts us of sin. He illuminates Scripture. He unveils Christ more fully. This is why prayer and the Word of God must go hand in hand. As we meditate on Scripture, the Spirit brings it to life. As we pray, the Spirit reminds us of what we have read. The Spirit connects the Word to our situation, our emotions, our struggles.

When we pray apart from the Spirit, we risk praying according to our own understanding. But when we pray in the Spirit, we are guided into a greater awareness of what God is doing in and through us.

Keeping in step with the Spirit requires listening

Galatians 5:25 says: *"Since we live by the Spirit, let us keep in step with the Spirit."* The phrase *"keep in step"* evokes the image of a soldier marching in rhythm, or a child learning to walk beside a parent. It requires attentiveness, alignment, and intentionality.

In prayer, this means listening as much as we speak. It means waiting before the Lord in silence. It means paying attention to the Spirit's gentle nudges, quiet convictions, and whispered reminders.

So much of our prayer life can become noise - lists of requests, repeated phrases, rushed devotions. But the Spirit invites us to a deeper rhythm. He teaches us to pause, to reflect, to receive. Elijah encountered the voice of God not in wind, fire, or earthquake - but in a gentle whisper (1 Kings 19:12).

That is often how the Spirit speaks. To keep in step with the Spirit in prayer means slowing down enough to hear His voice - and trusting Him enough to follow it.

The Spirit gives us boldness in prayer

The Spirit not only softens us - He strengthens us. He gives us boldness to come before God with confidence, not timidity. In Hebrews 4:16, we are told: *"Let us then approach God's throne of grace with confidence, so that we may receive mercy and find grace to help us in our time of need."*

This boldness comes from knowing we are loved, accepted, and empowered by the Spirit. It means we can pray with expectation, not fear. We can ask big things of a big God. We can intercede for others with passion and persistence.

The early church was marked by bold, Spirit-filled prayer. After Peter and John were threatened for preaching, the believers gathered and prayed: *"Enable your servants to speak your word with great boldness."* (Acts 4:29). They were not intimidated by persecution - they were emboldened by the Spirit. And verse 31 tells us: *"After they prayed, the place where they were meeting was shaken. And they were all filled with the Holy Spirit and spoke the word of God boldly."* The Spirit-filled life produces a prayer life of courage and confidence.

Prayer as partnership with the Spirit

To walk in the Spirit is to pray in the Spirit. And to pray in the Spirit is to live in the Spirit. We cannot separate our prayer life from our spiritual life. They are woven together. One fuels the other. Let us not settle for a prayer life that is mechanical, shallow, or self-directed. Let us press into the deep waters of Spirit-led prayer - prayer that listens, learns, yields, trusts, and obeys.

Ask yourself today:

➢ Am I keeping in step with the Spirit in my prayer life?
➢ Do I pause to listen, or only rush to speak?
➢ Do I rely on the Spirit's guidance, or try to manufacture the right words?
➢ Do I allow prayer to shape my character, my responses, and my desires?

The Holy Spirit has not only come to empower your service or sanctify your heart - He has come to transform your prayers. Will you let Him lead?

The Call to persevering prayer

By now in our book, we've seen that prayer is not simply a spiritual discipline - is a way of life, a relational response to our Father, and a Spirit-empowered journey. In this final part of this chapter on *"The Holy Spirit and Prayer,"* we turn to one of the greatest challenges in the Christian life: persevering in prayer.

Why do so many of us begin prayerfully but struggle to persist? Why do our prayers often grow faint over time? Why is it so difficult to keep praying when the answers don't come? The answer lies partly in our human frailty - but more deeply, it points to our need for supernatural help. We need the Holy Spirit not only to begin praying, but to continue praying when we feel tired, discouraged, or spiritually dry. The good news is this: The Holy Spirit sustains us in prayer. He empowers us to endure, fuels our hope, strengthens our resolve, and intercedes when we cannot. Let's explore how.

Prayer requires endurance - and the Spirit provides It

The Apostle Paul, writing from prison, urged the church in Ephesus to live as warriors - not with swords or shields, but with the full armour of God. And what was the final piece of this armour? *"And pray in the Spirit on all occasions with all kinds of prayers and requests. With this in mind, be alert and always keep on praying for all the Lord's people."* (Ephesians 6:18).

Note that Paul not only says to *"pray in the Spirit,"* but also to *"always keep on praying."* He understood that prayer was a long-haul activity, not a short burst. True spiritual warfare is sustained by ongoing, Spirit-empowered prayer. In our flesh, we grow weary. Our enthusiasm fades. Our minds wander. But the Spirit strengthens us to endure. He supplies the inner fire to keep returning to the Father's presence, even when we feel nothing, see nothing, and hear nothing.

Jesus urged persistent prayer

Jesus Himself told a parable in Luke 18:1-8 to show the value of perseverance in prayer: *"Then Jesus told his disciples a parable to show them that they should always pray and not give up."* In this parable, a persistent widow keeps pleading with an unjust judge until he finally grants her request - not because he cares, but because she refuses to stop asking. Jesus draws a striking contrast: if even an unjust judge can be moved by persistence, how much more will our loving Father respond to His children who cry out to Him day and night?

The parable ends with a sobering question: *"However, when the Son of Man comes, will he find faith on the earth?"* (v.8). In other words: will He find people who are still praying? Persevering in prayer is one of the greatest signs of faith. It's the Holy Spirit who cultivates that faith within us, even when we don't feel strong.

The Spirit sustains us in seasons of silence

There are times when prayer feels like talking to a wall. No answers come. The heavens seem silent. Our words feel empty. But in those difficult moments, the Spirit is not absent - He is always working silently, strengthening deeply, and interceding faithfully. Romans 8:26 reminds us: *"In the same way, the Spirit helps us in our weakness. We do not know what we ought to pray for, but the Spirit himself intercedes for us through wordless groans."* Even when your heart is too heavy to speak, your spirit too tired to pray, the Holy Spirit is praying on your behalf. You are never voiceless in the throne room of heaven - the Spirit carries your burden there continually.

The Spirit gives hope as we wait

Persevering in prayer often means waiting. And waiting is hard - especially when we are desperate for healing, restoration, provision, or clarity. But here's what the Spirit does: He fills us with hope even as we wait. Romans 15:13 offers this blessing: *"May the God of hope fill you with all joy and peace as you trust in him, so that you may overflow with hope by the power of the Holy Spirit."* Hope is not wishful thinking - it is the Spirit-given assurance that God is good, that He hears, and that His timing is perfect. The Holy Spirit helps us trust God's heart even when we cannot see His hand.

The Spirit intercedes through us for others

One of the most selfless acts in the Christian life is to intercede for others. This kind of prayer is often laborious, especially when the need is great, the situation is dire, or the answers are slow. Paul described Epaphras in Colossians 4:12: *"Epaphras... is always wrestling in prayer for you, that you may stand firm in all the will of God."*

Wrestling in prayer is tiring work - but it is work the Spirit empowers and honours. Intercession is not a burden we carry alone. The Spirit groans with us, stirs compassion within us, and teaches us how to plead according to God's will. If we try to carry the burdens of others without the Spirit's help, we will be crushed. But with the Spirit, we are always strengthened for the long haul.

The Spirit reignites a cold prayer life

Many believers, if they're honest, go through dry seasons in prayer. They feel distant from God. Their prayers feel routine, shallow, or lifeless. But the Spirit is a fire-starter. He specializes in revival - not just in churches, but in hearts. Paul told Timothy: *"For this reason I remind you to fan into flame the gift of God, which is in you…"* (2 Timothy 1:6). The Spirit can rekindle what has grown cold. He can stir fresh desire, deepen our hunger, and awaken a longing for God again. Sometimes, all it takes is a simple, honest prayer: *"Holy Spirit, help me pray again."* And He will.

The Spirit empowers us to finish well

The Christian life is a race - and prayer is part of the daily rhythm that keeps us running. But the Spirit does not merely start us on the race - He helps us finish. Paul wrote in 2 Timothy 4:7: *"I have fought the good fight, I have finished the race, I have kept the faith."*

No true believer finishes that race well without the sustaining presence of the Holy Spirit. He is the fuel, the guide, the strength, and the encouragement to keep going - and to keep praying - until the end. When your body is weary, your heart is heavy, and your soul is dry, the Spirit whispers truth, brings Scripture to mind, and reminds you of the Father's faithfulness.

Conclusion: Don't stop praying - The Spirit won't

To persevere in prayer is not merely to try harder - it is to trust deeper. It is to lean on the Spirit who is already praying within you, beside you, and through you. You will face distractions, disappointments, and delays. But the Holy Spirit will not stop praying. And if you yield to Him, neither will you.

Let me close this chapter with this encouragement from Paul, *"Be joyful in hope, patient in affliction, faithful in prayer."* (Romans 12:12) Faithfulness in prayer is not a product of strong will - it is a gift of the Spirit to those who ask.

So ask Him: *"Holy Spirit, sustain me in prayer. Keep me seeking, trusting, and waiting. Help me persevere when I'm tired. Teach me to pray when I'm dry. Carry my groans when I have no words. And lead me to the Father, again and again."* And He will.

15. 'THE PSALMS: OUR PRAYER BOOK'

The Psalms - God's prayer book

The Psalms are one of the richest treasures in all of Scripture. For thousands of years, they have served as the prayer book of God's redeemed people. Whether sung aloud in temple worship or whispered in the darkness of exile, the Psalms have given language to the full range of human experience - joy and sorrow, praise and lament, faith and doubt.

Jesus quoted the Psalms more than any other Old Testament book. On the cross, He prayed some words from Psalm 22: *"My God, my God, why have you forsaken me?"* (Matthew 27:46). After His resurrection, He explained to His disciples how *"everything must be fulfilled that is written about me in the Law of Moses, the Prophets and the Psalms."* (Luke 24:44). If The Lord's Prayer is the model prayer - teaching us how to pray - the Psalms are the prayer workshop - teaching us what to pray, how to feel, and how to bring our whole selves before God. In this chapter, we will begin to explore how the Psalms can shape our prayer lives by helping us speak honestly, lament deeply, and worship fully.

The Psalms teach us to pray honestly

One of the most striking features of the Psalms is their raw honesty. There's no religious pretence. No spiritual performance. The psalmists speak from the gut - expressing fear, confusion, anger, and even despair, all before the face of God. Psalm 13 begins with this gut-wrenching cry: *"How long, Lord? Will you forget me forever? How long will you hide your face from me?"* (v.1). These are not polite words. They are really desperate. Honest. Unfiltered. And yet, they are included in Scripture - which means God welcomes this kind of prayer.

Sometimes, we think prayer must be cleaned up - that we need to present a polished version of ourselves. But the Psalms remind us that God does not require perfection in our prayers. He desires truth. Psalm 51:6 declares: *"Yet you desired faithfulness even in the womb; you taught me wisdom in that secret place."*

Psalm 145:18 adds: *"The Lord is near to all who call on him, to all who call on him in truth."* When we pray the Psalms, we learn to drop the mask. We learn to come as we are, not as we think we should be. God is not offended by our honesty - He is drawn to it.

The Psalms give us words when we have none

There are times when we want to pray but simply don't know what to say. Our emotions are too heavy, our minds too clouded, our hearts too weary. In those moments, the Psalms become our voice.

Psalm 42:3-5 *"My tears have been my food day and night, while people say to me all day long, 'Where is your God?' These things I remember as I pour out my soul: how I used to go to the house of God under the protection of the Mighty One with shouts of joy and praise among the festive throng. Why, my soul, are you downcast? Why so disturbed within me? Put your hope in God, for I will yet praise him, my Saviour and my God."*

In this one psalm, we see sorrow, confusion, memory, longing, and hope mingled together. That is what prayer often looks like - a mix of brokenness and belief. When we pray the Psalms, we allow Scripture to give voice to our silence. We learn that prayer is not always neat or predictable - it is often messy and meandering, just like life.

The Psalms lead us into lament

Modern Western Christianity often struggles with lament. We prefer celebration to sorrow, clarity to confusion, victory to vulnerability. But the Psalms show us that lament is a vital part of prayer. Over one-third of the Psalms are laments - cries of anguish, complaint, protest, and grief. And yet, they are still prayers of faith. To lament is not to doubt God - it is to bring our pain to Him, believing He is the only one who can help.

Here is a beautiful example from Psalm 6:6-7, *"I am worn out from my groaning. All night long I flood my bed with weeping and drench my couch with tears. My eyes grow weak with sorrow; they fail because of all my foes."*

This kind of prayer may feel foreign to us, but it is deeply biblical. Lament is a bridge between suffering and hope. It allows us to grieve honestly while still clinging to God's promises. When we suppress lament, we risk suppressing our humanity. But when we pray the laments of the Psalms, we discover that God meets us in our sorrow - not to shame us, but to sustain us.

The Psalms move us from despair to praise

Though many Psalms begin in lament, they rarely end there. Most of them take a turn - a moment when the psalmist, after pouring out his heart, remembers who God is and responds in praise. Psalm 13, which began with *"How long, Lord?"* ends like this: *"But I trust in your unfailing love; my heart rejoices in your salvation. I will sing the Lord's praise, for he has been good to me."* (Psalm 13:5–6). This is not denial - the pain is still real - but it is anchored by hope.

The Psalms teach us that worship is not a denial of reality but a declaration of trust. When we learn to pray like the psalmists, we learn to let pain and praise exist side by side. We can weep and worship in the same breath.

The Psalms are for every season of life

Perhaps the greatest gift of the Psalms is their incredible breadth. They meet us in every stage and every season of life.

> ➤ In times of gratitude, we have psalms of thanksgiving (Psalm 100, 103)
> ➤ In times of awe, we have psalms of praise (Psalm 8, 19, 148)
> ➤ In times of guilt, we have psalms of confession (Psalm 32, 51)
> ➤ In times of fear, we have psalms of trust (Psalm 23, 27)
> ➤ In times of anger, we have psalms of complaint (Psalm 10, 74)
> ➤ In times of confusion, we have psalms of wisdom (Psalm 1, 119)
> ➤ In times of longing, we have psalms of desire (Psalm 42, 63, 84)

Whatever you're facing, there is a Psalm for you. The Psalms are not just poetry - they are divinely inspired prayers that help us navigate the full complexity of human emotion in the presence of God.

The Psalms: Our companions in prayer

As we begin this new direction in our book, we invite the Psalms to be our companions in prayer. These ancient songs are not outdated relics - they are Spirit-breathed sincere expressions of the human heart crying out to God.

➤ If you're new to prayer, start with the Psalms.
➤ If you're weary in prayer, return to the Psalms.
➤ If you've lost your words, borrow the Psalms.
➤ If your heart is full, sing the Psalms.
➤ If your soul is crushed, weep with the Psalms.

And as you do, remember that Jesus prayed these words, too. He lived them, fulfilled them, and invites us to join Him in this holy conversation. Now we will look more deeply at how the Psalms shape our theology of God, and how they teach us to address Him as Father, King, Shepherd, and Deliverer.

Our view of God shapes our prayers

We have just explored how the Psalms help us pray honestly and deeply - giving us a language for every season of life. Now, we turn to another crucial aspect of prayer: the God to whom we pray. Our prayers are always shaped by our vision of God. If we see Him as distant, we will pray cautiously. If we see Him as angry, we will pray fearfully. If we see Him as weak, we will pray hopelessly. But if we see Him as He truly is - powerful, loving, faithful, and near - our prayers will reflect trust, reverence, and intimacy.

The Psalms don't just teach us how to pray - they reveal to us who God is. In poetic and personal language, the psalmists paint a rich portrait of God's character.

They show us that God is not an abstract force or an aloof deity - He is Father, Shepherd, King, Refuge, and Redeemer. Let us now walk through some of these central images of God in the Psalms and discover how they can completely transform the way we pray.

God as Shepherd - Our tender guide

Perhaps the most beloved psalm in all of Scripture is Psalm 23. It begins with this well-known line: *"The Lord is my shepherd, I lack nothing."* (Psalm 23:1). This opening statement is more than poetic - it is deeply theological. In ancient Israel, a shepherd was responsible for feeding, protecting, guiding, and caring for the sheep. To say *"The Lord is my shepherd"* is to say: God sees me, knows me, and provides for me personally.

Psalm 23 is a prayer born out of trust: *"Even though I walk through the darkest valley, I will fear no evil, for you are with me; your rod and your staff, they comfort me."* (Psalm 23:4). This is not distant theology - it is intimate relationship.

The psalmist is not praying to an idea of God, but to the God who walks with him through the darkest valleys. When we pray with Psalm 23 in mind, our hearts are reminded that we are never alone. We can speak with confidence, knowing our Shepherd leads us.

God as refuge - Our safe place in trouble

The Psalms are filled with declarations of God as refuge - a shelter in the storm, a fortress in battle, a safe place when the world is falling apart.

Psalm 46 opens with these words: *"God is our refuge and strength, an ever-present help in trouble. Therefore we will not fear, though the earth give way and the mountains fall into the heart of the sea..."* (Psalm 46:1-2). In this chaotic world, where health can fail, relationships can fracture, and security can disappear overnight, we need a place to hide - and the Psalms remind us of that God Himself is our hiding place.

Psalm 91 echoes this promise: *"Whoever dwells in the shelter of the Most High will rest in the shadow of the Almighty."* (Psalm 91:1). This view of God shapes our prayers. When we feel threatened, we don't need to panic or run to other sources of comfort. We run to God our refuge, praying with confidence that He will shield and sustain us.

God as King - Ruler over all

While many Psalms are personal, others lift our eyes to the cosmic rule of God as King over all the earth. Psalm 47:7–8 declares: *"For God is the King of all the earth; sing to him a psalm of praise. God reigns over the nations; God is seated on his holy throne."* When the world feels chaotic and evil seems to be winning, the Psalms remind us that God is sovereign. He is not surprised by human rebellion. He is not shaken by political upheaval. His throne is not up for election.

This has a direct impact on our prayers. We can pray with boldness because we know God has the power to act. We can intercede for nations, leaders, and situations far beyond our control - because they are not beyond His. Psalm 2 captures both the rebellion of the nations and the sure reign of God: *"Why do the nations conspire and the peoples plot in vain? The One enthroned in heaven laughs; the Lord scoffs at them."* (Psalm 2:1,4). This may seem harsh, but it is actually reassuring: no enemy, no force, no kingdom can thwart the purposes of our God. To pray with a vision of God as King is to pray with reverence, but also with confidence.

God as Father - compassionate and close

Though the Psalms predate Jesus' full revelation of God as Father, they still contain glimpses of God's paternal care. Psalm 103:13 gives us this powerful picture: *"As a father has compassion on his children, so the Lord has compassion on those who fear him."* And verse 14 adds: *"For he knows how we are formed, he remembers that we are dust."* This is the God we come to in prayer - not a tyrant, not a critic, not an accuser, but a compassionate Father who understands our frailty.

Jesus would later teach us to pray, *"Our Father in heaven…"* - but the foundation for this intimacy was already laid in the Psalms. When you feel weak, sinful, or unworthy to pray, remember: your heavenly Father is full of mercy. He does not demand perfection before He listens. He invites honesty, humility, and dependence. Psalm 145:18 assures us: *"The Lord is near to all who call on him, to all who call on him in truth."*

God as redeemer – the One Who saves

At the heart of the Psalms is a deep awareness of human sin - and an even deeper confidence in God's mercy. Psalm 130 is a beautiful example: *"If you, Lord, kept a record of sins, Lord, who could stand? But with you there is forgiveness, so that we can, with reverence, serve you."* (Psalm 130:3-4). And in Psalm 103: *"Praise the Lord, my soul, and forget not all his benefits - who forgives all your sins and heals all your diseases, who redeems your life from the pit…"* (Psalm 103:2-4). These psalms remind us that we do not earn access to God in prayer. We come because He redeems us. He forgives, restores, and renews. Our prayers are not transactions to win His favour - they are responses to His grace.

So often, our struggles in prayer are not because we lack technique - but because we lack a clear vision of who God is. The Psalms correct our distortions and expand our understanding. Is your view of God too small? Is He distant in your imagination? Is He angry or uninterested? Is He too much like you - or not enough? Let the Psalms reintroduce you to the God who is:

➢ Shepherd – gently leading you.
➢ Refuge – hiding you in His presence.
➢ King – reigning over all.
➢ Father – caring for you with compassion.
➢ Redeemer – forgiving and restoring you.

To pray the Psalms is to let God reshape our theology with every line we utter. It is to allow Scripture to inform not only what we pray, but to whom we pray - and how we trust Him.

Now let me explore how the Psalms might shape our prayers in community, helping us intercede for others, worship together, and unite our hearts before God as His people.

Prayer is not just personal - It's communal

As we conclude our focus on Praying the Psalms, we now shift from the personal to the communal. Many of us instinctively view prayer as a private, individual experience - and rightly so. Jesus taught us to go into our rooms and pray in secret (Matthew 6:6). But biblical prayer is not limited to individual expression. It is also something the people of God do together.

The Psalms are filled with prayers not just for me, but for us - the community, the nation, the people of God. In fact, the Psalms were Israel's corporate prayer book. They were sung and prayed in public worship, on pilgrimages, in festivals, and in the Temple. They shaped the prayer life of a whole people, not just individuals. Let's examine how the Psalms guide our prayers as a body of believers - helping us pray for unity, for God's blessing on others, for the healing of nations, and for joy in our shared spiritual journey.

The Psalms call us to pray as a people

Psalm 122 begins with a joyful communal invitation: *"I rejoiced with those who said to me, 'Let us go to the house of the Lord.'"* (v.1). This is not a solitary voice - it is a collective one. The psalmist rejoices with others as they go together to worship. Their destination is the same. Their hearts are united in purpose.

Verse 6 continues: *"Pray for the peace of Jerusalem: 'May those who love you be secure.'"* Here, the people are urged to pray not just for themselves, but for the peace and wellbeing of the entire city of God. This is intercession on a grand scale - a vision of prayer that goes beyond the personal and embraces the community. In a fragmented and individualistic age, the Psalms remind us that the heart of prayer is not me-centred but God-and-others-centred. The Lord's Prayer itself is plural: *"Our Father ... give us ... forgive us ... lead us ... deliver us."*

The Psalms lead us to pray for unity

Psalm 133 is a short but powerful picture of community: *"How good and pleasant it is when God's people live together in unity!"* (Psalm 133:1). Unity is not uniformity - it is the beauty of diverse people gathered around the presence of God with a shared heart and mission. This Psalm likens unity to oil flowing down Aaron's beard and to the dew of Hermon - both images of abundance, life, and divine blessing. When we pray the Psalms, we learn to value the unity of the Church. We learn to pray not just for our own preferences or experiences, but for the shared health of the body of Christ. It's easy to focus on ourselves in prayer. But the Psalms pull us outward - toward the needs, struggles, and joys of those around us.

The Psalms teach us to intercede for the nations

Psalm 67 is a striking example of intercessory prayer that extends far beyond the borders of Israel: *"May God be gracious to us and bless us and make his face shine on us - so that your ways may be known on earth, your salvation among all nations."* (Psalm 67:1-2). This prayer isn't just for God's blessing - it's for that blessing to become a channel through which the whole world can sees and know our God.

Verse 3 continues: *"May the peoples praise you, God; may all the peoples praise you."* This is the heartbeat of intercession - not just asking for God to meet our needs, but for His glory to spread, His salvation to be known, His praise to rise from every nation. The Psalms stretch our vision. They teach us to pray for what is bigger than us - for the global Church, for unreached people, for justice and peace across the earth.

The Psalms help us pray for revival and restoration

There are seasons when God's people feel spiritually dry or morally compromised. The Psalms give us words for these moments - prayers that seek renewal and restoration. Psalm 85 begins with gratitude for past mercies: *"You, Lord, showed favour to your land; you restored the fortunes of Jacob."* (Psalm 85:1).

But it quickly moves into a heartfelt plea for present revival: *"Will you not revive us again, that your people may rejoice in you?"* (Psalm 85:6). This is the language of collective longing. It's not *"revive me,"* but *"revive us."* The psalmist is interceding for the whole community - that they might return to joy, holiness, and intimacy with God.

Praying the Psalms teaches us that we are not only responsible for our own spiritual lives – we are all participants in the spiritual health of our church, our city, and our nation. When we see complacency, compromise, or decline, the Psalms equip us to cry out with bold, biblical hope: *"Restore us, O God!"* (Psalm 80:3)

The Psalms call us to celebrate together

Not all communal prayer is intercession. The Psalms also lead us in shared rejoicing. Psalm 126 is a wonderful celebration of God's deliverance - and a declaration of joy that is contagious: *"Our mouths were filled with laughter, our tongues with songs of joy. Then it was said among the nations, 'The Lord has done great things for them.'"* (Psalm 126:2)

Prayer is not always lament. Sometimes it is sheer joy. And when God moves in mighty ways, the right response is not silent gratitude but public praise. The Psalms also teach us to celebrate together, to remember together, and to laugh together. They remind us that testimony fuels worship. When God delivers one of us, all of us rejoice. This is what it means to be the Church - to carry each other's burdens and also share each other's victories.

The Psalms train our hearts for worshipful prayer

Corporate prayer isn't just about asking - it's also about adoration. The Psalms are full of invitations to worship: *"Come, let us sing for joy to the Lord; let us shout aloud to the Rock of our salvation. Let us come before him with thanksgiving and extol him with music and song."* (Psalm 95:1–2). Notice the collective language: *"let us sing ... let us come ... let us extol."* The Psalms invite us not only to pray for one another, but to praise together - lifting a unified voice of honour to our King.

Conclusion: The Psalms shape a praying community

We've seen that the Psalms are not only a personal devotional guide - but they are also a communal prayer manual.

They teach us to:

➤ Pray with others.
➤ Pray for others.
➤ Pray as a people.
➤ Pray toward God's global purposes.

They stretch our hearts beyond our personal needs and draw us into the shared life of God's people. And in doing so, they make us more like Christ - who Himself intercedes for us at the right hand of God (Romans 8:34).

As we pray the Psalms together, we find ourselves knit together in worship, in grief, in hope, and in praise. Let us not neglect the gift of communal prayer. Let us recover the Psalms as a voice for the Church, a way to unite our hearts, strengthen our faith, and glorify our God.

16. 'PRAYING LIKE JESUS'

Learning prayer from the One Who needed none

When we think about Jesus, we often focus on His teaching, His power, His miracles, or His death and resurrection. But perhaps one of the most overlooked aspects of His life is also one of the most profound - Jesus was a man of prayer.

This is staggering when you think about it. Jesus was the sinless Son of God. He was in perfect fellowship with the Father. He lacked nothing in wisdom, power, or holiness. And yet, He prayed constantly. If Jesus needed prayer - how much more do we?

In this chapter, we begin an exploration of the prayer life of Jesus. We'll focus first on His habit of prayer - how, when, and why He prayed. This will help us understand that prayer is not a religious duty, but a relational necessity. Then we will explore His content in prayer, followed by His intercession for His followers.

Jesus prayed frequently

From the beginning to the end of the Gospels, we see Jesus praying. Luke 5:16 says: *"But Jesus often withdrew to lonely places and prayed."* That small verse reveals so much to us. Jesus had a demanding ministry. Crowds followed Him. The sick lined up for healing. The religious leaders questioned His every move. And yet - He withdrew to pray. Luke doesn't say this happened once. He says it happened often.

In Mark 1:35, we can see this discipline clearly: *"Very early in the morning, while it was still dark, Jesus got up, left the house and went off to a solitary place, where he prayed."*

This was after a full day of ministry in Capernaum, healing many and casting out demons. Most of us, after a day like that, would have slept in. But Jesus rose early to be alone with the Father. Prayer was not an optional activity for Jesus - it was essential to His mission.

Jesus prayed before major decisions

Another pattern we see in the Gospels is that Jesus prayed before significant moments. Just before choosing the twelve apostles, we read: *"One of those days Jesus went out to a mountainside to pray and spent the night praying to God. When morning came, he called his disciples to him and chose twelve of them, whom he also designated apostles."* (Luke 6:12–13). Jesus didn't just pray for a moment. He prayed through the night. He was about to appoint the men who would carry the gospel to the world after His death. He sought the Father's wisdom with intensity and surrender.

This challenges our often-casual approach to making decisions. How many times do we rush into choices - relationships, careers, commitments - without seeking God in prayer? Jesus shows us that prayer is not just for crises. It's for clarity, direction, and alignment with the will of the Father.

Jesus prayed in times of suffering

One of the most intimate and powerful examples of Jesus' prayer life is in the Garden of Gethsemane.

Matthew 26:36–39 *"Then Jesus went with his disciples to a place called Gethsemane, and he said to them, 'Sit here while I go over there and pray.' He took Peter and the two sons of Zebedee along with him, and he began to be sorrowful and troubled. Then he said to them, 'My soul is overwhelmed with sorrow to the point of death. Stay here and keep watch with me.' Going a little farther, he fell with his face to the ground and prayed, 'My Father, if it is possible, may this cup be taken from me. Yet not as I will, but as you will.'"*

This is not a ceremonial prayer - this is raw, anguished surrender. Jesus, fully human, recoiled at the horror of the cross. But He brought that agony to the Father in prayer. This scene teaches us that it's not unspiritual to struggle. Even Jesus struggled - but He struggled in prayer. He didn't avoid God; He went deeper into communion with Him. When we suffer, we are often tempted to isolate ourselves from God. But the way of Jesus is different. He teaches us to bring our sorrow, confusion, and fear into prayer - and to entrust ourselves fully to the will of God.

Jesus prayed in times of gratitude and joy

Jesus didn't only pray in crisis. He also prayed in thanksgiving and joy. In Matthew 11:25, He says: *"I praise you, Father, Lord of heaven and earth, because you have hidden these things from the wise and learned, and revealed them to little children."* This spontaneous praise erupts after His teaching on the kingdom. Jesus is overjoyed that the truth of God is being revealed to the humble and not the proud. His instinct is to pray.

In John 11:41, before raising Lazarus from the dead, He prays publicly: *"Father, I thank you that you have heard me. I knew that you always hear me…"* Even in miraculous moments, Jesus turns to the Father in gratitude. His prayer life was not driven only by need, but by delight. This reminds us that prayer should be rooted not just in desperation, but in adoration. It is good and right to praise God in prayer, to thank Him, to enjoy Him.

Jesus taught others to pray by example

One of the most powerful ways that Jesus taught was through example. In Luke 11:1, we read: *"One day Jesus was praying in a certain place. When he finished, one of his disciples said to him, 'Lord, teach us to pray, just as John taught his disciples.'"* Notice - they didn't ask Him how to perform miracles. They didn't ask Him how to preach. They asked Him how to pray. Why? Because they saw Him praying. They saw the power and peace that flowed from His relationship with the Father.

Jesus didn't only exhort us to pray. He modelled prayer every day and night - and that model had a lasting impact. The early Church became a praying community because its foundation was built on the prayer life of its Master.

Jesus prioritised solitude and stillness

One of the most repeated themes in Jesus' prayer life is His intentional withdrawal from people and noise. Luke reminds us: *"Jesus often withdrew to lonely places and prayed."* (Luke 5:16). He didn't always pray in public. He carved out space for stillness, for silence, for intimacy.

In our extremely noisy, hyperconnected world, this example is revolutionary. If the Son of God needed solitude to pray - how much more do we? Too often, our prayers are squeezed into the margins of our lives - a hurried thought before a meal or a quick word before bed. But Jesus scheduled prayer. He built it into His rhythm. He knew that the life of the Spirit requires space - not just for speaking, but for listening.

The invitation to pray like Jesus

The prayer life of Jesus Christ is not just an inspiration - it's an invitation. He does not merely show us what is possible - He draws us into that same relationship. Through the Holy Spirit, we are invited to join Jesus in His unbroken fellowship with the Father.

Hebrews 5:7 *"During the days of Jesus' life on earth, he offered up prayers and petitions with fervent cries and tears to the one who could save him from death, and he was heard because of his reverent submission."*

This is the Jesus who prays for us. This is the same Jesus who teaches us to pray. In the next part of this chapter, we'll explore the content of Jesus' prayers - what He prayed for, how He prayed for others, and what that reveals about His heart and mission. For now, may we be inspired and challenged by the rhythm of Christ's life - a rhythm grounded in prayer, sustained by prayer, and always surrendered in prayer.

Listening to the prayers of the Son

In Part 1, we looked at the prayer habits of Jesus - how frequently, privately, and fervently He prayed. In this message, we turn from His practice to His priorities in prayer. What did Jesus actually pray for? What filled His heart when He spoke to the Father?

To truly learn how to pray, it is not enough to observe Jesus at prayer - we must listen to the content of His prayers. What He prayed reveals what He valued, what burdened His heart, and what He wanted for those who followed Him.

When we pay attention to Jesus' prayers, we discover a pattern of selflessness, intimacy, and mission. His prayers were not long lists of personal desires. They were focused on the Father's glory, the needs of others, and the advancing of God's kingdom. Let's now listen closely to the prayer life of our Lord.

Jesus prayed for the glory of the Father

The longest recorded prayer of Jesus is in John 17. Often referred to as the High Priestly Prayer, it is a sacred moment just before His betrayal and arrest. And how does He begin? *"After Jesus said this, he looked toward heaven and prayed: 'Father, the hour has come. Glorify your Son, that your Son may glorify you.'"* (John 17:1). This is not a selfish request. Jesus is asking that His suffering and death - *"the hour"* - would result in the glorification of the Father through the obedience of the Son.

In verse 4, Jesus says: *"I have brought you glory on earth by finishing the work you gave me to do."* Jesus' greatest desire in prayer was that the Father would be glorified. His entire life - and His prayer life - was about God's glory, not His own comfort or success. This challenges us. How often are our prayers shaped by that same goal? Do we pray first for God's name to be honoured, His will to be done, His kingdom to come? Jesus teaches us that prayer begins with adoration and alignment.

Jesus prayed for His disciples' protection

In John 17:11, Jesus turns His focus to His followers: *"Holy Father, protect them by the power of your name, the name you gave me, so that they may be one as we are one."* Jesus knew the trials His disciples would face. He knew the persecution, confusion, and temptation that would follow His death.

So He prayed for their protection - not just physical, but spiritual protection. He repeats this plea in verse 15: *"My prayer is not that you take them out of the world but that you protect them from the evil one."* This is a beautiful and realistic prayer. Jesus doesn't ask for escape - He asks for strength. He knows His people must remain in the world, but He prays that they would be kept safe within it.

This encourages us to pray for one another's endurance in the face of spiritual warfare. Jesus sets a precedent for intercessory prayer - asking the Father to guard our hearts from the schemes of the enemy.

Jesus prayed for unity among believers

Unity is one of the most repeated themes in John 17. Jesus prays not only for the twelve disciples, but for all future believers - that is, us: *"My prayer is not for them alone. I pray also for those who will believe in me through their message, that all of them may be one, Father, just as you are in me and I am in you."* (vv.20-21).

This is astonishing. In His final hours, Jesus prayed for our unity. He didn't pray for our buildings, budgets, or programmes. He prayed that we would be one, just as the Father and Son are one. Why? Verse 21 continues: *"...so that the world may believe that you have sent me."*

Our unity is a witness. It shows the world the reality of Christ. When we love each other, forgive each other, and work together, we reflect the heart of the Triune God. This should guide our prayers for the Church today. Instead of merely praying for our personal needs, let us ask for deeper unity, greater harmony, and the healing of divisions in the body of Christ.

Jesus prayed for His disciples to be sanctified

Still in John 17, Jesus also prays for the spiritual growth of His followers: *"Sanctify them by the truth; your word is truth."* (v. 17). To be sanctified is to be made holy - to be set apart for God's purposes Jesus wants His disciples to be more than just protected; He wants them to be transformed.

He doesn't pray that they would merely survive, but that they would become holy through the truth of God's word. This teaches us to pray not only for comfort or solutions, but for growth. We should be praying for one another's character, for increased love, faith, patience, and purity. Jesus shows us that the aim of prayer is not just relief - it's refinement.

Jesus prayed for the success of His mission

Jesus prayed with a global vision. In John 17:18, He says: *"As you sent me into the world, I have sent them into the world."* Jesus saw His disciples as missionaries. He prayed that they would be faithful in carrying His message, just as He had been faithful in delivering the Father's. Later in verse 23, Jesus again connects the unity of believers with the credibility of the mission: *"Then the world will know that you sent me and have loved them even as you have loved me."*

Jesus' prayers were saturated with missional passion. He was not focused only on the people before Him - He prayed for those who were still far off. This calls us to enlarge the scope of our prayers. Do we pray for the lost? Do we pray for boldness in evangelism, for labourers in the harvest field, for God's name to be known in every nation?

Jesus prayed for the faith of individuals

Jesus didn't only pray globally or generally - He often prayed for specific individuals with love and concern. In Luke 22, Jesus tells Peter: *"Simon, Simon, Satan has asked to sift all of you as wheat. But I have prayed for you, Simon, that your faith may not fail. And when you have turned back, strengthen your brothers."* (vv.31-32). Jesus foresaw Peter's denial, but He also saw his restoration. He didn't pray that Peter wouldn't fall - He prayed that Peter's faith would survive the fall.

This shows us the tender, personal heart of Jesus. He knows our frailty. He intercedes not to preserve our performance, but our faith. There are times when we may feel like we're being *"sifted as wheat."* But we can take heart in this truth: Jesus prays for us (see Hebrews 7:25). And when others go through trials, we too can pray that their faith would not fail.

Jesus prayed for God's will to be done

Perhaps the most difficult and beautiful prayer Jesus ever prayed is found in Gethsemane: *"My Father, if it is possible, may this cup be taken from me. Yet not as I will, but as you will."* (Matthew 26:39).

This prayer is incredibly raw with emotion. Jesus was facing betrayal, torture, and death. He honestly asked if there was another way. But He ended His prayer with complete surrender. He didn't just pray what He felt - He prayed what He believed. He trusted the Father's will more than His own feelings. This is perhaps the most challenging kind of prayer - and the most transformative. When we pray, *"Your will be done,"* we are not giving up; we are giving in to a higher wisdom, a greater love.

Praying like Jesus means praying for others

In Jesus' prayers, we see a beautiful pattern:

- ➢ He prays for God's glory above all else.
- ➢ He prays for others - their protection, unity, and sanctification.
- ➢ He prays for the mission - that the world may know.
- ➢ He prays with trust - surrendering to the will of the Father.

To pray with Jesus is to move from self-centred requests to God-centred intercession. It is to align our hearts with His - full of compassion, vision, and truth. As we grow in prayer, may our words begin to echo His. May our prayers become less about our comfort and more about God's kingdom.

Jesus is still praying!

When we think of Jesus' ministry, we often focus on what He did - His teaching, healing, death, and resurrection. But Scripture reveals something astonishing: Jesus is still ministering. Right now. And one of His key ministries is prayer. The risen, ascended Lord Jesus is not inactive. He is seated at the right hand of the Father, interceding for us. This is not symbolic language - it is a glorious truth that grounds our confidence and invites us to join Him in a life of prayer.

Before wrapping up this chapter, I want to now explore the intercessory role of Jesus - what He continues to do for us - and how we are called to partner with Him in interceding for others.

As we draw our focus to Christ's heavenly ministry, we will discover both comfort and calling. Jesus prays for us - and calls us to pray with Him.

Jesus lives to intercede for us

Hebrews 7:25 is one of the most remarkable verses in all of Scripture: *"Therefore he is able to save completely those who come to God through him, because he always lives to intercede for them."* Not only did Jesus die for us, He now lives for us - with a very specific purpose: intercession. This is not a passive existence. Jesus is actively bringing our needs before the Father. He is our Advocate, our Great High Priest, our Mediator. He knows our struggles, and He speaks on our behalf.

Romans 8:34 echoes this: *"Who then is the one who condemns? No one. Christ Jesus who died - more than that, who was raised to life - is at the right hand of God and is also interceding for us."* Jesus' intercession means we are never alone in our prayers. When we falter, He prays. When we forget, He remembers. When we fall, He pleads. This is not meant to make us passive, but hopeful. Jesus is never indifferent to our weakness - He always intercedes through it.

Jesus intercedes as One Who understands us

Hebrews 4:15–16 gives us this assurance: *"For we do not have a high priest who is unable to empathize with our weaknesses, but we have one who has been tempted in every way, just as we are - yet he did not sin. Let us then approach God's throne of grace with confidence, so that we may receive mercy and find grace to help us in our time of need."* Jesus' intercession is not mechanical. It is empathetic. He understands. He has been where we are. He knows the pull of temptation, the weight of sorrow, the weariness of ministry, and the agony of betrayal.

When He prays for us, it is not from a distance. It is from personal experience. This gives us confidence to pray. We are not coming to a cold deity, but to a compassionate Saviour who gets it - and who speaks to the Father on our behalf.

Jesus intercedes for our faith

In Luke 22:31-32, Jesus says something deeply personal to Simon Peter: *"Simon, Simon, Satan has asked to sift all of you as wheat. But I have prayed for you, Simon, that your faith may not fail. And when you have turned back, strengthen your brothers."*

Jesus knew Peter would deny Him. He knew he would weep bitterly. But He also knew Peter would return. Why? Because Jesus had prayed for his faith. Jesus did not pray that Peter would be perfect. He prayed that Peter would endure. This is a beautiful reminder that Jesus' intercession is not just for our performance - but for our perseverance. We often feel unworthy to pray. But Jesus prays that our faith, not our failures, will define us.
Jesus calls us to join Him in intercession

Jesus doesn't just intercede for us - He invites us to intercede with Him. 1 Timothy 2:1 urges us: *"I urge, then, first of all, that petitions, prayers, intercession and thanksgiving be made for all people."* We are called to pray for others - not just ourselves. This is a direct continuation of Jesus' ministry. Paul models this beautifully in Colossians 1:9: *"For this reason, since the day we heard about you, we have not stopped praying for you."* He intercedes constantly for the believers, just as Christ does.

To pray with Jesus is to take up the ministry of intercession. This means we step into the gap on behalf of others. We pray for their salvation, healing, restoration, and growth. We weep with those who weep, and we plead with God for their sake.

Intercessory prayer is an act of love

The greatest thing you can do for someone is pray for them. Why? Because in prayer, we bring them before the One who knows them perfectly, loves them fully, and can transform them eternally. *"The prayer of a righteous person is powerful and effective."* (James 5:16). This is not just a platitude - it is a promise. Your prayers really make a difference. When you pray for someone's encouragement, strength, healing, or breakthrough, you are aligning yourself with the intercession of Christ.

We live in a world that is hurting. People often feel unseen and unloved. When we say, *"I'm praying for you,"* we are saying, *"You matter to God - and to me."* Intercessory prayer is not a religious obligation. It is an act of love.

Intercession changes the one who prays

When we intercede for others, we are not only blessing them - we are being changed ourselves. Prayer bends the heart toward compassion. It removes bitterness. It breaks pride. It quiets judgment. It opens us to God's heart for others.

When Job prayed for his friends - the very same friends who had misunderstood and accused him, something incredibly powerful happened: *"After Job had prayed for his friends, the Lord restored his fortunes and gave him twice as much as he had before."* (Job 42:10). God worked through Job's intercession - and also in Job's heart. Intercession is one of the greatest tools God uses to make us more like Jesus.

Intercession is a ministry of hope

To intercede is to hope - to believe that change is possible, that healing can come, that salvation is near. Abraham interceded for Sodom. Moses interceded for Israel. Daniel interceded for his nation. Paul interceded for the Church. And Jesus intercedes for us all. This ministry is not just for pastors or prayer warriors - it is for every believer. Are there prodigals in your life? Intercede.

Are there broken marriages around you? Intercede. Are there unreached people in the world? Intercede. Is your church facing challenges? Intercede. Intercession is how we bring the brokenness of the world into the presence of its Healer.

Conclusion: The invitation to join Jesus in prayer

Jesus is praying for you - right now. He is your advocate, your friend, your intercessor. Hebrews 7:25 declares that He *"always lives to intercede."* That is His current occupation - and it will never cease. The question is not whether Jesus is praying - the question is: will we pray with Him?

To follow Jesus is to be a person of intercession - someone who lifts others up in prayer, who stands in the gap, who believes God for more.

Let us draw near with confidence.

Let us pray boldly, consistently, and compassionately.

Let us join Jesus in His unceasing, unstoppable, loving ministry of intercession. He is praying - and He is calling us.

Will you answer Him today?

17. 'PERSEVERING PRAYER'

The challenge of consistent prayer

Prayer is a gift. But sometimes it feels like a battle. We start with passion and intention. We long to spend time with God, to pour out our hearts, and to hear His voice. But as time passes, distractions come, answers seem delayed, and enthusiasm can fade. We find ourselves struggling - not just to pray, but to keep praying. Jesus anticipated this very struggle. Perseverance in prayer is not a natural human tendency. It must be taught, practiced, and encouraged. In this chapter, we will explore what it means to persist in prayer, even when God seems silent, circumstances seem unchanged, and our hearts feel weary.

Jesus taught us to pray without giving up

The parable of the persistent widow is one of the most clear and direct teachings of Jesus about perseverance in prayer. *"Then Jesus told his disciples a parable to show them that they should always pray and not give up."* (Luke 18:1). The story that follows is about a widow who keeps coming to an unjust judge pleading her case. The judge doesn't care about people or God, but he eventually gives in because she keeps bothering him. Jesus concludes with this powerful promise: *"Will not God bring about justice for his chosen ones, who cry out to him day and night?"* (Luke 18:7)

Jesus contrasts the heartless judge with our loving Father. If persistence can move even an unjust man, how much more will our prayers be heard by the One who delights in us? This parable tells us that persistence is not about changing God's mind, but about demonstrating our trust in God's character.

Prayer is an act of Faith, not just a task

When we pray and do not receive answers straight away, our natural reaction may be to doubt - not just the outcome, but sometimes even the point of prayer. But prayer is never pointless. Paul writes in Colossians 4:2: *"Devote yourselves to prayer, being watchful and thankful."*

To devote yourself to something is to persist in it, to refuse to quit, even when it's difficult. We don't pray only when we feel like it. We pray because it is an act of faith - a declaration that God is real, He is listening, and He is working. Romans 12:12 urges believers to: *"Be joyful in hope, patient in affliction, faithful in prayer."* Why must we be faithful in prayer? Because God often works in ways and on timelines that we cannot see. If we only pray when the results are immediate, we will quickly give up. But if we trust in His character, we will continue to pray - because He is worthy, regardless of the outcome.

Delay is not denial

One of the most common reasons people give up on prayer is this: they waited, and nothing happened. But in God's economy, delay is not denial. Think of Abraham and Sarah, waiting for a child. Or Hannah, pouring out her soul for a son. Or the Israelites crying out in Egypt for deliverance. In each case, the delay was long - sometimes painfully so - but the answer eventually came. Psalm 27:14 encourages us: *"Wait for the Lord; be strong and take heart and wait for the Lord."* Waiting is not passive. Biblical waiting involves active trust - continuing to believe, continuing to pray, continuing to lean into God, even when the timeline stretches longer than we hoped. Jesus delays are never wasted. They often develop in us the very thing we need most: dependence.

When Heaven is silent, keep praying

There are times when prayer feels like a one-sided conversation. We speak, we cry, we beg - and heaven seems silent. David experienced this too. In Psalm 13, he wrote: *"How long, Lord? Will you forget me forever? How long will you hide your face from me?"* (Psalm 13:1). These are honest words. There's no pretending here. David felt abandoned - but he kept talking to God. Even in his confusion and despair, he kept the conversation going. That is perseverance.

The end of the Psalm shows the shift that prayer brings: *"But I trust in your unfailing love; my heart rejoices in your salvation. I will sing the Lord's praise, for he has been good to me."* (Psalm 13:5–6).

The circumstances hadn't changed. But David had. And that's often the effect of prayer - it changes us *before* it changes our situation.

Perseverance grows our spiritual maturity

When we persist in prayer, we are being shaped by the Spirit. James 1:4 says: *"Let perseverance finish its work so that you may be mature and complete, not lacking anything."* That also includes perseverance in prayer.

When we keep showing up in the secret place - even when we're tired, distracted, disappointed, or discouraged - we are being spiritually formed. God is not just interested in giving us what we ask for. He is interested in forming us into the image of Christ.

Jesus Himself prayed persistently. In the Garden of Gethsemane, knowing the suffering to come, He prayed three times - not to avoid pain, but to submit to the Father's will. Each prayer was an act of surrender. Each time, He rose with renewed strength. Perseverance in prayer teaches us resilience, humility, patience, and trust - the hallmarks of Christian maturity.

The role of the Church in encouraging perseverance

One of the great supports in persevering prayer is community. The early church gathered to pray regularly and persistently. In Acts 1:14, we read: *"They all joined together constantly in prayer."*

In Acts 12:5 we read, *"So Peter was kept in prison, but the church was earnestly praying to God for him."* That word earnestly implies continual, fervent, unrelenting prayer. The church didn't gather once and give up. They prayed until the miracle came.

We need that kind of community today. When our own faith falters, we need others to lift us up. When someone else is discouraged, we can be their strength. Persevering prayer is not only a personal discipline – it is also a shared rhythm in the life of the whole church.

Don't give up!

Luke 18:1 remains the anchor of this chapter: *"Then Jesus told his disciples a parable to show them that they should always pray and not give up."* This is not a suggestion - it is a loving command. Jesus knows how prone we are to lose heart. He knows that prayer often feels unrewarded. And so He gives us the gift of this story - the widow who refused to give up, and the Judge who eventually responded.

But God is not like that judge. Our Father is good, generous, and attentive. If we, His children, continue to cry out to Him, He will respond - in His time, and in His way. So take heart today. If your prayers feel weak, keep praying. If heaven seems silent, keep praying, don't stop. If the answer seems delayed, keep praying. Perseverance in prayer is not about eloquence or power - it's about faithfulness.

When prayer feels like a burden

Every Christian who takes prayer seriously will, at some point, experience weariness. We pray and wait, pray and plead, pray and groan - and it can feel like we're pouring water into a cracked jar. Nothing seems to stay. Nothing seems to change. And we grow tired. If that's you, you're not alone. Even the most faithful intercessors have felt this weight. In fact, the deeper your love, the heavier your prayers may feel. Love makes us vulnerable. It compels us to pray for people, churches, and nations in crisis. But the longer we carry those burdens, the more exhausting it can become. This part of our chapter explores how to persevere when we are burdened - and how to stay faithful in intercession when answers are slow, when the load is heavy, and when our strength runs out.

Do not grow weary in doing good - even in prayer

Galatians 6:9 gives us this encouragement: *"Let us not become weary in doing good, for at the proper time we will reap a harvest if we do not give up."* This applies just as much to prayer as to outward service. Prayer is doing good. When we intercede for others, we are sowing into their lives and into God's kingdom.

The results may not be immediate, but the promise remains: *"at the proper time we will reap a harvest."* Satan wants us to quit before that time comes. He whispers:

➢ *"You've prayed enough."*
➢ *"It's not making a difference."*
➢ *"God has already decided."*
➢ *"You're wasting your breath."*

But Scripture answers: *"Do not give up."* Every prayer sown in faith is a seed planted in God's field. And He is faithful to bring fruit in His time.

When God says, "Not Yet," trust His timing

There's a profound story in Luke 11:5–8, where Jesus speaks of a man going to a friend at midnight to ask for bread. The friend at first refuses: *"Don't bother me. The door is already locked, and my children and I are in bed."* But Jesus says: *"I tell you, even though he will not get up and give you the bread because of friendship, yet because of your shameless audacity he will surely get up and give you as much as you need."* (Luke 11:8)

The Greek word translated *'shameless audacity'* is quite often rendered as *persistence*. The image is one of bold, unrelenting appeal. This is not a polite whisper at the door - it's determined, persistent, knocking. Jesus then says: *"So I say to you: Ask and it will be given to you; seek and you will find; knock and the door will be opened to you."* (Luke 11:9). These verbs: *ask, seek, knock* - are in the present continuous tense in the Greek. They mean: keep on asking, keep on seeking, keep on knocking. Why? Because often the first answer is *"Not yet."* This doesn't mean *"No."* It simply means *"Keep coming."* God is not reluctant, but He is very wise.

Strength in weakness: When prayer feels beyond us

There are times when we pray with all our might - and still feel utterly weak. Paul experienced this. We see in 2 Corinthians 12, where he pleaded with God to remove a *"thorn in the flesh."*

Three times he asked, and the final answer came: *"My grace is sufficient for you, for my power is made perfect in weakness."* (12:9). Paul's response? *"Therefore I will boast all the more gladly about my weaknesses, so that Christ's power may rest on me."* Sometimes God answers by changing the situation. Other times, He answers by strengthening us to endure it. That is still an answer. When we feel too tired to keep praying - when our hearts are heavy and our words run dry - God's strength takes over.

Romans 8:26 says: *"In the same way, the Spirit helps us in our weakness. We do not know what we ought to pray for, but the Spirit himself intercedes for us through wordless groans."* We are not alone in our intercession. Even when we have no words, the Spirit groans with us and for us.

How to persevere in intercession for others

One of the hardest aspects of prayer is long-term intercession for others, especially when there is little visible progress. You may be praying for a wayward child, an unbelieving friend, a broken marriage, or a sick loved one. You've prayed for weeks, months, maybe even years. The silence is deafening. What keeps us going? Love. Love refuses to give up. It clings to hope. It believes God is working even when we can't see it.

1 Corinthians 13:7 says that love: *"always protects, always trusts, always hopes, always perseveres."* When our strength fails, love compels us to keep praying. And love reminds us that we are not the saviour - God is. Our job is not to fix people. It is to bring them to the One Who can. That's what intercession is. It is not about eloquence. It is about faithfulness.

Refreshing the weary soul in prayer

How do we renew our strength when we feel exhausted praying?

1. *Return to the Word.* God speaks through Scripture. When we feel dry, reading His promises revives us. Psalm 119:28 says: *"My soul is weary with sorrow; strengthen me according to your word."*

2. *Change your environment.* Go for a walk. Write out your prayers. Sing instead of speaking. Kneel, stand, lie down - shift your posture. Sometimes a small change in setting can reawaken your spiritual focus.

3. *Invite others in.* Don't carry your burdens alone. Share with a trusted friend or prayer partner. James 5:16 tells us: *"Therefore confess your sins to each other and pray for each other so that you may be healed."*

4. Praise even when you don't feel like it. Praise shifts your focus from your problems to God's power. It lifts your eyes. Even in lament, you can say: *"Yet I will praise him, my Saviour and my God."* (Psalm 42:11)

The promise that keeps us going

Jesus never promised prayer would be easy. But He did promise it would be heard. In Luke 18:7–8, He said: *"And will not God bring about justice for his chosen ones, who cry out to him day and night? Will he keep putting them off? I tell you, he will see that they get justice, and quickly."*

This promise reminds us of two things:

➢ God hears the cries of His children.
➢ He will act in His perfect time.

Until that time comes, we persevere.

Keep Knocking

Are you tired of praying? Is your faith wearing a little thin? Jesus understands. And He calls you to keep knocking. The doors of heaven are not closed to the weary - they are open wide. The One on the other side is not reluctant. He is loving, patient, and present. Let this truth sink deep into your soul: *"Those who hope in the Lord will renew their strength."* (Isaiah 40:31).

I also want us to look at how this perseverance in prayer shapes our character, strengthens community, and advances God's purposes in the world. Just remember, you are not alone.

The Spirit helps you. The Son intercedes for you. And the Father waits to answer. So keep praying ... keep believing and keep knocking.

More than a spiritual discipline

As we conclude this chapter on persevering in prayer, we move from the struggle of prayer to its fruit. Persevering in prayer is not just about getting answers - it's about what God does in us as we wait. Prayer is not a vending machine. Prayer is not a contract. Prayer is a relationship. And like every meaningful relationship, it grows and deepens over time - especially through seasons of silence, testing, and perseverance. When we commit to persistent prayer, something profound happens. Our whole character is transformed. Our relationship with God matures. Our heart becomes more aligned with heaven. And through us, the world begins to shift. Let's explore the powerful fruit that grows in the soil of faithful, persevering prayer.

Persevering prayer shapes our character

One of the great by-products of persistent prayer is spiritual maturity. Romans 5:3-5 says: *"Not only so, but we also glory in our sufferings, because we know that suffering produces perseverance; perseverance, character; and character, hope. And hope does not put us to shame, because God's love has been poured out into our hearts through the Holy Spirit."* Although Paul is writing here about suffering, the principle applies to all forms of waiting and perseverance - including prayer. As we persist, we grow. We become more patient, more hopeful, more humble, and more compassionate. Persistent prayer strips away self-reliance. It confronts our need for control. It teaches us to trust even when we don't understand. And as we lean into God, we begin to reflect Him.

Prayer builds intimacy with God

Matthew 6:6 gives us one of the most intimate pictures of prayer: *"But when you pray, go into your room, close the door and pray to your Father, who is unseen. Then your Father, who sees what is done in secret, will reward you."*

There is something sacred about the private place of prayer. When no one else sees, no one applauds, no one affirms - God is present. And He sees. When we persevere in prayer over the long haul, we discover a deeper fellowship with God than we could have imagined. He becomes not just the one who answers prayers, but the One who walks with us through the waiting. Psalm 27:8 reflects this heart: *"My heart says of you, 'Seek his face!' Your face, Lord, I will seek."* The more we seek God's hand (what He can do), the more we are drawn to seek His face (who He is). Prayer then becomes less about getting things from God and more about being with God. That's spiritual intimacy.

Prayer that changes the world

Persevering prayer doesn't only change us - it can change the world. James 5:16–18 says: *"The prayer of a righteous person is powerful and effective. Elijah was a human being, even as we are. He prayed earnestly that it would not rain, and it did not rain on the land for three and a half years. Again he prayed, and the heavens gave rain, and the earth produced its crops."* James' point here is simple but profound: ordinary people, when they pray, can often release some extraordinary results. Elijah wasn't superhuman. He was just committed. He prayed earnestly. And heaven responded.

We too can pray in faith, not because of our power, but because of God's power working through our persistent faithfulness. Jesus taught us to pray, *"Your kingdom come, your will be done, on earth as it is in heaven."* That is a call to partner with God in ushering in His purposes. And perseverance is required - because the kingdom does not come through one-off prayers. It comes through ongoing, consistent intercession.

The cumulative power of prayer

One of the great mysteries of the Christian life is this: some breakthroughs only come after persistent, layered prayer. In Revelation 5:8, we get a glimpse into the heavenly reality: *"Each one had a harp and they were holding golden bowls full of incense, which are the prayers of God's people."* Your prayers don't vanish. They are stored. Collected. Treasured.

The imagery here is beautiful: heaven gathers our prayers like incense - fragrant, precious, rising before God's throne. And when the time is right - God acts. This is not manipulation. It's participation.

God in His sovereignty has chosen to work through our prayers. So we must not despise the days, weeks, months - or even years - of prayer that seem unanswered. In God's economy, nothing is wasted.

Persistent prayer aligns us with God's will

Another fruit of perseverance in prayer is alignment. Over time, as we keep praying, our focus begins to shift. We may start praying, *"Lord, change this situation,"* but we end up praying, *"Lord, change me."* Or we begin by praying for something specific - and eventually realise we were asking for the wrong thing. Jesus Himself modelled this in Gethsemane: *"My Father, if it is possible, may this cup be taken from me. Yet not as I will, but as you will."* (Matthew 26:39).

Persevering in prayer is not about persuading God to do our will - it's about being conformed to His. When we stick with it, when we keep returning to the place of prayer, something shifts. We stop trying to control outcomes, and we start surrendering. We learn to trust that God's way is always best, even when we don't understand it.

God rewards those Who seek Him

Hebrews 11:6 assures us: *"And without faith it is impossible to please God, because anyone who comes to him must believe that he exists and that he rewards those who earnestly seek him."* God is a rewarder. Not a wage-giver - but a generous, joyful Father who honours those who earnestly seek Him.

Sometimes the reward is the very thing we've prayed for. Other times, the reward is a transformed heart, a deeper intimacy, a clearer understanding of His will, or a supernatural peace.

Philippians 4:6-7 captures this beautifully: *"Do not be anxious about anything, but in every situation, by prayer and petition, with thanksgiving, present your requests to God. And the peace of God, which transcends all understanding, will guard your hearts and your minds in Christ Jesus."* That peace - which doesn't always come with a "yes" - is itself a divine reward.

Your prayers matter - Even when you don't see the result

One of the hardest realities of persevering prayer is this: we don't always live to see the fruit. But that doesn't mean the prayers were in vain. Hebrews 11 recounts the stories of people who lived by faith, prayed by faith, and died in faith - without receiving the fullness of what was promised.

In Hebrews 11:39-40). *"These were all commended for their faith, yet none of them received what had been promised, since God had planned something better for us..."* Some of the prayers you're praying now may be answered in your children's lifetime. Or in generations yet to come. Your intercession may be shaping things beyond your own horizon. But God sees. And God remembers.

Conclusion: The legacy of persevering prayer

As we bring this message to a close, let's remember that the greatest prayers in history were not always dramatic or eloquent. They were faithful. They were whispered in bedrooms, shouted in deserts, groaned in hospital rooms, and wept over prodigal children. Persistent, fervent prayer, even when nothing seemed to change. And through those prayers, heaven was touched and earth was changed.

May we be that kind of people. People who pray - and keep praying. Who seek - and keep seeking. Who knock - and keep knocking. Because our Father is good. And He hears. And He will answer.

18. 'A LEGACY OF PRAYER'

More than a ritual

As we reach the final chapter in this book on The Lord's Prayer and the life of prayer it inspires, we turn our attention now to a joyful reality that undergirds it all: *prayer is communion*. Not merely a ritual, not only a request - but a relationship. Prayer is the living breath of ongoing fellowship with the living God.

In this closing chapter, I want to explore what it means to abide in God daily - to walk with Him, talk with Him, and delight in Him every moment. Because at its heart, the life of prayer is not a religious duty but a relational delight. As Jesus said, *"I am the vine; you are the branches. If you remain in me and I in you, you will bear much fruit; apart from me you can do nothing."* (John 15:5). That is a perfect image of communion: remaining, dwelling, abiding in Christ.

Jesus invites us to abide

In John 15:4, Jesus gives a clear and beautiful invitation: *"Remain in me, as I also remain in you."* To *"remain"* or *"abide"* in Christ is to maintain an unbroken connection. It is a posture of continual dependence, trust, and nearness. Abiding is not a once-a-day appointment with God. It's not a devotional box to tick. It is a life posture - a way of being. This is what prayer becomes when it matures: not a task, but a way of life.

Paul echoes this in 1 Thessalonians 5:16-18 when he offers us the secret of living the Lord's Prayer: *"Rejoice always, pray continually, give thanks in all circumstances; for this is God's will for you in Christ Jesus."* These aren't three separate commands – they're a picture of a life lived in communion with God.

To *"pray continually"* does mean just mumbling prayers 24/7. It means maintaining a continual awareness of and connection to the presence of God - speaking with Him, listening for Him, depending on Him, in every situation. This is abiding.

The joy of daily fellowship

Psalm 16:11 captures the joy of communion with God: *"You make known to me the path of life; you will fill me with joy in your presence, with eternal pleasures at your right hand."* So often, we associate prayer with burden, discipline, or even guilt. But the psalmist reminds us that the presence of God is the place of joy.

When we begin to see prayer not as a burden but a joy, not as a task but a treasure, we will find ourselves drawn to God not out of duty, but out of desire. This doesn't mean every prayer time is euphoric. But it means there is a deep, abiding gladness in walking with God. Just as a vine gives life to its branches, God gives life, strength, and joy to those who remain in Him.

Abiding through the day: Practising God's presence

Brother Lawrence, a 17th-century monk, became known for his ability to "practice the presence of God." He didn't just pray in the chapel; he prayed while cooking, cleaning, and working. He wrote: *"The time of business does not with me differ from the time of prayer; and in the noise and clatter of my kitchen, I possess God in as great tranquillity as if I were upon my knees at the blessed sacrament."*

This is the vision of abiding – it is not escaping life to pray, but inviting God into all of life. What does that look like?

➢ Whispering prayers in traffic.
➢ Giving thanks while washing dishes.
➢ Asking God for wisdom before a meeting.
➢ Praising Him during a walk.
➢ Listening for His nudge in conversations.

Prayer becomes a rhythm, a pulse, a heartbeat beneath all we do. And in that rhythm, joy grows.

Remaining in Christ in a distracted world

Of course, we live in a noisy world. Distraction is everywhere. Abiding is not easy at all - especially in a culture that prizes multitasking and busyness.

Remaining in Christ takes intentionality. Jesus says in John 15:10: *"If you keep my commands, you will remain in my love."* Obedience is a key to abiding. As we walk in His ways, our hearts remain tender and tuned to His voice.

Another key is attention. Psalm 16:8 says: *"I keep my eyes always on the Lord. With him at my right hand, I will not be shaken."* To abide is to choose focus - to train our hearts and minds to return, again and again, to God. That may mean:

➤ Setting reminders to pause and pray.
➤ Carving out silence each day.
➤ Learning to turn worry into prayer.
➤ Cultivating gratitude.

It's not about perfection - it's all about persistence.

The fruit of abiding prayer

Jesus gives us a beautiful promise in John 15:7: *"If you remain in me and my words remain in you, ask whatever you wish, and it will be done for you."* This isn't a blank cheque - it's actually a statement of alignment. When we abide in Christ, His desires become our desires. His will becomes our will.

So we begin to pray not selfishly, but in harmony with His heart. And when that happens, prayer becomes powerful. Jesus continues: *"This is to my Father's glory, that you bear much fruit, showing yourselves to be my disciples."* (John 15:8) Fruit is the natural result of connection. We don't need to strive or strain - we simply need to remain. Abiding always produces the fruit of prayerful communion with God.:

➤ *Love*: because we are filled with God's love.
➤ *Joy*: because His presence is our delight.
➤ *Peace*: because we trust His care.
➤ *Patience*: because we are rooted in eternity.
➤ *Faithfulness*: because He is always faithful to us.

The invitation to ongoing communion

At this point in this final chapter, we need to hear Jesus' gentle and powerful call again: *"Remain in me, as I also remain in you."* The life of prayer is not a box to check - it is a vine to cling to, a presence to dwell in, a Saviour to walk with. Just let this truth rest in your heart: You are invited into a life of continual communion with the God who loves you. And in His presence, there is fullness of joy.

Fellowship with God, fellowship with one another

We have explored the joy of abiding in Christ - of prayer as an ongoing, joyful communion with God. But this life of prayer is never isolated. When we walk in communion with the Father, that intimacy inevitably overflows into our relationships with others. True spiritual communion is both vertical (with God) and horizontal (with others). The deeper we go with God, the wider our hearts open toward our neighbours, our brothers and sisters in Christ, and even our enemies. Let's now explore how abiding in Christ transforms our community life, shapes our love for one another, and reflects the unity that Jesus Himself prayed for.

Communion with God creates fellowship with others

John writes in 1 John 1:3: *"We proclaim to you what we have seen and heard, so that you also may have fellowship with us. And our fellowship is with the Father and with his Son, Jesus Christ."* And in verse 7: *"But if we walk in the light, as he is in the light, we have fellowship with one another."*

Notice the flow: fellowship with God leads to fellowship with others. Prayer is not just about personal spirituality; it's also about shared life. When we walk closely with God, we become more patient, more compassionate, more gracious - because we are being shaped by the One who is love.

That's why the early church devoted themselves not only to prayer but also to fellowship (Acts 2:42). These weren't separate experiences - they were part of the same shared life in Christ.

Abiding in Christ means loving one another

Jesus connects the abiding life to love in John 15:12, *"My command is this: Love each other as I have loved you."* He follows with the powerful statement: *"Greater love has no one than this: to lay down one's life for one's friends."* (v.13) When we remain in Christ, we begin to love like Christ. This isn't just a feeling - it's a sacrificial, servant-hearted love. It shows up in how we speak to each other, serve one another, forgive one another, and stand with one another. In verse 17, Jesus then repeats the command: *"This is my command: Love each other."* Our prayers may be eloquent. Our theology may be sound. But if we are not growing in love, we are not truly abiding.

Love in community: Philippians 2 and the mind of Christ

Paul describes what this love looks like in Philippians 2:1-4: *"Therefore if you have any encouragement from being united with Christ, if any comfort from his love, if any common sharing in the Spirit... then make my joy complete by being like-minded, having the same love, being one in spirit and of one mind."* He continues: *"Do nothing out of selfish ambition or vain conceit. Rather, in humility value others above yourselves, not looking to your own interests but each of you to the interests of the others."*

Here we can see the outworking of communion: unity, humility, selflessness, mutual care. And this flows not from effort alone, but from being *"united with Christ."* The more we commune with Him, the more His mind becomes ours. This is why a truly praying community is not just pious - it is loving.

How prayer transforms our relationships

Persistent, joyful communion with God reshapes how we relate to others in at least three ways:

a) *It softens our hearts:* When we spend time in God's presence, we become more aware of our own faults and more gracious toward others. We become slow to anger, quick to forgive, eager to understand.

b) *It grows compassion:* Communion with God opens our eyes to the pain around us. We begin to see others as He sees them. We are moved to intercede, to serve, to speak life.

c) *It builds bridges:* Prayer tears down walls - between cultures, generations, personalities. As we pray for others, we begin to love them. And love makes room.

The Church as a fellowship of communion

In Acts 2:42-47, we see a beautiful portrait of the early Church: *"They devoted themselves to the apostles' teaching and to fellowship, to the breaking of bread and to prayer."* The result? *"All the believers were together and had everything in common. They broke bread in their homes and ate together with glad and sincere hearts."*

This was not mere social activity. It was the overflow of their shared communion with Christ. The Church was never meant to be a collection of individual spiritual consumers. It is a body, a family, a fellowship rooted in Jesus. When we pray together, worship together, confess together, give together - we participate in a divine communion.

The Communion Table: a shared meal of fellowship

At the heart of Christian worship is the Lord's Table - Communion. Jesus said: *"This is my body, broken for you… This cup is the new covenant in my blood."* (1 Corinthians 11:24-25). When we take communion, we are not only remembering Christ's death - we are also participating in deep, shared fellowship with Him and with one another.

Paul warns the Corinthian church not to treat the Lord's Supper lightly. Why? Because it is a sacred moment of unity. To eat and drink in division is to miss the point. The Table reminds us:

➤ We are forgiven people.
➤ We are united people.
➤ We are one body, with many members.

Prayer that builds community

A Church that prays together becomes a church that grows together. Prayer in community:

➤ Builds trust.
➤ Deepens intimacy.
➤ Breaks down isolation.
➤ Connects hearts.

When we carry one another's burdens before the Lord, we grow closer - not just to God, but to each other. James 5:16 says: *"Therefore confess your sins to each other and pray for each other so that you may be healed."* That kind of vulnerability only flows from deep trust, and that trust is forged in shared prayer.

Let communion overflow

As we live in daily communion with God, let that communion overflow into our homes, our churches, and our relationships. Let us become people who:

➤ *Abide in Christ* through every moment of the day.
➤ *Love one another* as He has loved us.
➤ *Build churches* marked by prayerful unity and shared life.

The joy of communion is not just for the secret place - it is for every place, every conversation, every act of service, every gathering of believers. As Jesus said in John 15:11: *"I have told you this so that my joy may be in you and that your joy may be complete."* May your joy be full. May your fellowship be rich. May your life of prayer never end.

Communion that never ends

As we bring this chapter book to its conclusion, we turn our gaze toward the ongoing journey of prayer - a journey that begins in this life and continues into eternity. Prayer is not just for the hard days, or the sacred moments. Prayer is for life - life with God now and forever.

We have spoken much of intimacy, discipline, intercession, and worship. But beneath all these lies a deeper truth: communion with God is eternal. What begins now in faith and prayer will one day be fulfilled in glorious presence.

So this final chapter is about learning to live in unceasing communion with God - both in the ordinary moments of life and in the great hope of eternity.

Devoted to ongoing prayer

Colossians 4:2 says: *"Devote yourselves to prayer, being watchful and thankful."* The word *"devote"* here implies persistence, priority, and passion. This isn't just casual or occasional - it is intentional, consistent, heartfelt communion with God. This verse captures three core aspects of the prayer life of a believer:

➤ *Devotion:* Prayer is not a side activity; it is central.
➤ *Watchfulness:* We stay alert to God's movements, purposes, and answers.
➤ *Thankfulness:* Gratitude fuels and frames our conversation with God.

Paul doesn't just recommend prayer. He calls us to devotion. Not because God needs our prayers - but because we need His presence. This devotion shapes absolutely everything. It informs our attitudes, touches our relationships, and controls our many reactions. We begin to live not in panic or distraction, but in constant communion with our loving Father.

Prayer in the everyday rhythm of life

Romans 12:12 gives a succinct pattern: *"Be joyful in hope, patient in affliction, faithful in prayer."* This isn't advice for a church service. It's for life. It's how we navigate the highs and lows, the waiting seasons, the breakthroughs.

To be faithful in prayer means we don't let go of God, regardless of the circumstances. It means prayer becomes our default, our anchor, our rhythm.

This is what we see in the lives of biblical saints:

➤ *Daniel* prayed three times a day, even under threat of death.

➤ *David* poured out his heart in the psalms - in joy, sorrow, anger, and praise.

➤ *Jesus* withdrew regularly to be with the Father, often before dawn or late into the night.

Their lives teach us that prayer is not a formula but a lifestyle. And that's what we are called into - a prayerful, Spirit-filled way of life.

When prayer becomes real presence

Something mysterious happens the more we live in prayer: we begin to recognise God's nearness in everything. We notice His handiwork in creation. We sense His peace in stillness. We hear His whisper in Scripture. We feel His prompting in conversation. Prayer no longer feels like something we start and stop. It becomes our awareness of His presence, even when we're not speaking.

This is what Paul means when he says in 1 Thessalonians 5:17 *"Pray continually."* Prayer is not a burden. It is a gift - the gift of walking moment by moment with our Saviour. This posture helps make us more attuned, more surrendered, more joyful - because we know we are never alone.

Communion at the table - and beyond

One of the most beautiful pictures of communion is found in Luke 24:30–32, where the risen Jesus walks with two disciples on the road to Emmaus. *"When he was at the table with them, he took bread, gave thanks, broke it and began to give it to them. Then their eyes were opened and they recognized him, and he disappeared from their sight."* And they said to each other: *"Were not our hearts burning within us while he talked with us on the road and opened the Scriptures to us?"*

That moment - the breaking of bread, the opening of eyes - captures what communion is meant to be. Not just an event, but an awakening. Their hearts burned because Jesus was with them. When we learn to live in prayerful communion, our hearts will burn too. Not with anxiety or fear, but with love, revelation, and joy. Every conversation becomes sacred. Every meal becomes worship. Every act of kindness becomes a prayer. Because God is with us.

Communion that leads to mission

One of the great themes of the Bible is that communion leads to commission. Moses spoke with God face-to-face - and then was sent to Pharaoh. Isaiah saw the Lord high and exalted - and then heard, *"Whom shall I send?"* Jesus communed with the Father - and then said, "As the Father has sent me, I am sending you." So too for us.

Prayer is not escape from the world - it is equipping for it. The deeper we go with God in the secret place, the more ready we are to step into the public place - not with pride, but with power; not with fear, but with faith. When we live in communion, we carry the presence of God into the world - into our homes, our workplaces, our neighbourhoods. We become walking prayers, living testimonies, tangible evidence of the kingdom.

The eternal future of communion

Revelation 21:3-4 gives us a clear glimpse of the ultimate joy of communion: *"And I heard a loud voice from the throne saying, 'Look! God's dwelling place is now among the people, and he will dwell with them. They will be his people, and God himself will be with them and be their God. He will wipe every tear from their eyes. There will be no more death or mourning or crying or pain, for the old order of things has passed away.'"*

This is where the story is heading - not toward disconnection, but toward perfect communion. No more barriers. No more silence. No more distance. Just God with us, forever. The life of prayer we practice now is a foretaste of that eternal reality.

Every quiet moment, every whispered prayer, every encounter in the Spirit - it's a glimpse of the future. And the more we live in that communion now, the more we long for it fully.

The joy that sustains the journey

So how do we keep going? We keep going because we are not sustained by duty, we are sustained by delight. Psalm 16:11 reminds us: *"You make known to me the path of life; you will fill me with joy in your presence, with eternal pleasures at your right hand."* The presence of God is not a distant goal - it is our daily gift. And when we anchor ourselves in that joy, nothing can shake us.

➢ Not unanswered prayers.
➢ Not dark valleys.
➢ Not delayed promises.
➢ Not external pressure.

Because the joy of communion is stronger. It carries us. It lifts us. It draws us forward.

Conclusion: until we see Him face to face

And so we close this book not with an ending, but with a beginning. The Lord's Prayer has invited us into a new vision of prayer - one which is rooted in relationship, not religion; one which is sustained by grace, not striving. We've seen that:

➢ Prayer begins with knowing the Father.
➢ It embraces worship, surrender, trust, and petition.
➢ It sustains us in battle, in weakness, and in waiting.
➢ It grows us, transforms us, connects us to one another.
➢ And it prepares us for eternity.

So let us live this life of prayer - not out of obligation, but out of joy. Let us draw near daily. Let us walk in communion. Let us wait with hope for the day when prayer will no longer be needed because faith will become sight, and we will see Him face to face.

Until then, we pray: *"Our Father in heaven..."*

"I pray because I can't help myself. I pray because I'm helpless. I pray because the need flows out of me all the time, waking and sleeping. It doesn't change God. It changes me."

(C.S. Lewis)